KÖLSCH

The Classic Beer Style Series is devoted to offering in-depth information on world-class styles by exploring their history, flavor profiles, brewing methods, recipes, and ingredients.

OTHER BOOKS IN THE CLASSIC BEER STYLE SERIES

Brown Ale
Altbier
Barley Wine
Stout
Bock
Scotch Ale
German Wheat Beer
Belgian Ale
Porter
Oktoberfest, Vienna, Märzen
Lambic
Continental Pilsener
Pale Ale

KÖLSCH

History, Brewing Techniques, Recipes

Eric Warner

Classic Beer Style
Series no. 13

brewers publications

A Division of the
Brewers Association
Boulder, Colorado

Brewers Publications®
A Division of the Brewers Association
PO Box 1679, Boulder, CO 80306-1679
BrewersAssociation.org
BrewersPublications.com

Printed in the United States of America
10 9 8 7 6 5

ISBN-13: 978-0-937381-58-8
ISBN-10: 0-937381-58-6

Please direct all inquiries or orders to the above address.

Library of Congress Cataloging-in-Publication Data
Warner, Eric
     Kölsch : history, brewing techniques, recipes / Eric Warner.
        p. cm. — (Classic beer style series ; 13)
     Includes bibliographical references and index.
     ISBN 0-937381-58-6 (alk. paper)
     1. Beer—Germany—Cologne—History. 2. Brewing industry—
Germany—Cologne—History.   I. Title. II. Series.
TP577.W283   1998
641.2′3—dc21   98-28044
                                          CIP

To the small and regional brewers in Europe and North America. Be smarter, communicate your point of difference better, and, above all, always make the next batch your best.

Contents

Acknowledgments   *ix*

Introduction   *xi*

Chapter 1   *The Beer That Made Cologne Famous*   *1*

Chapter 2   *Sensory Profile and Chemical Composition*   *45*

Chapter 3   *Brewing Kölsch*   *63*

Chapter 4   *Fermentation, Maturation, and Packaging of Kölsch*   *89*

Chapter 5   *The Fun Part: Drinking Kölsch and Enjoying Cologne*   *103*

Chapter 6   *Recipes for the Hobby Brewer and the Professional*   *113*

Appendix A   *The Breweries of Cologne*   *129*

Appendix B   *Cologne's Classic Cuisine*   *157*

Appendix C   *Unit Conversion Chart*   *165*

Glossary   *167*

Bibliography   *199*

Index   *201*

About the Author   *217*

Acknowledgments

Thanks to Horst Dornbusch for providing technical assistance on this project, both in the form of direct input on the manuscript and lending me hard-to-find, out-of-print books written in German on the subject of Kölsch.

Another invaluable source of information was Detlef Rick. Mr. Rick is perhaps the biggest fan that Kölsch has. He works at the Dom Brauerei as a tour guide and public relations specialist and is currently writing a book of his own on Kölsch. Mr. Rick was kind enough to let me use his manuscript as a resource for mine. In particular, he has assembled thorough historical records of the Kölsch Konvention's member breweries. Without the use of these records I would not have been able to provide the depth of information about the Kölsch breweries. I wish Mr. Rick nothing but success with his forthcoming book and his quest to educate the German populace about the virtues of Kölsch.

I would also like to thank Michael Schneider of the Dom Brauerei. For one, he turned me on to Detlef Rick, and second, he provided me with a detailed historical account of the brewery as well as some of the photographs in this book.

Acknowledgments

Heinrich Becker and Reiner Radke of the Privatbrauerei Gaffel Becker & Co. also provided me with information not only regarding their brewery, but also on some of the brewing techniques used to brew Kölsch.

Most of the wonderful illustrations and images in this book came from *Kölsche Bier–und Brauhäuser*. Franz Mathar, coauthor of the book, was most helpful in providing the rights to use these images. If you can read German, his book is a must.

Finally, I would like to thank Theresa Duggan, Kim Adams, and Toni Knapp of Brewers Publications for their assistance and guidance in helping me keep this project going. I wish them continuing success in their publishing careers.

Introduction

Kölsch is the only language that one can also drink.

(Translated from the German)
—Anonymous

If you ask any knowledgeable beer drinker what country is best known for its lager beers, chances are "Germany" will be the answer. Likewise, if you ask that same person what the beer capital of Germany is, "Munich" will probably be the response. Twelve years ago, I would have boldly responded to those questions in the same manner. At that time, I was in Munich for a second visit to complete a degree at a brewing school, and I thought that German brewing was all about Bavaria's lagers and wheat beers. Sure, I had tried some of Germany's more obscure styles, such as Berliner *weiss* and *alt*, but why would anyone need to look any further than Bavaria to discover a wide array of beer styles and brands with which it would take the better part of a lifetime to become intimately familiar?

I remember being in one of my favorite student pubs when I found out about Kölsch. The pub manager was a Canadian-German with whom I had become friends, and he told me to try this new beer he had on tap. Since the vast majority of pubs and restaurants in Bavaria are controlled by large and small local breweries, it was always a pleasure to try something new at the independent pubs. When Fred poured me the glass of Kölsch, I said, "I'll order a full-sized one," and he replied that that was the full pour. The glass this beer was served in looked like a thimble next to the half-liter glasses that the Bavarians were using to drink *helles* and *weissbier*. Fred told me that these were the glasses he had received from the distributor for this particular beer. Being more knowledgeable than I was, Fred also told me that this was how it was done in Cologne.

Very well then, time to try the beer. The first thing that struck me was the thick, rocky head crowning the light-golden beer. Immediately I thought of helles and Pilsner, but when I tried the beer it seemed to be less malty than a helles and less bitter than a Pilsner. It also seemed to have a slightly more fruity character than either. It was soft and well balanced, with a relatively light body compared to the "big" beers of Bavaria. It was a wonderful surprise, and Fred had unknowingly made me a more frequent visitor to his pub.

The real experience with Kölsch was yet to come, however. At Fred's student pub all I knew about Kölsch was that it was a great, pale beer that was extremely enjoyable and easy to drink. On later visits to Cologne I would realize that Kölsch was actually an ale. What I also came to realize was that Kölsch was unique to Cologne and its neighboring townships and that it was protected by an appellation.

I was also about to find out more about the Kölsch culture. Kölsch is much more than just a beer style. It is a word for the German dialect spoken in Cologne and is used as an adjective to describe anything that has to do with Cologne, in much the same way that "German" is used to describe anything having to do with Germany. I also found out that the brewery did not send Fred some reject or close-out glassware with the kegs he ordered. The cylindrical, thin-walled, seven-ounce glasses were standard in every pub in Cologne. The two-centiliter glass was the only size in which my Kölsch was served. It seemed odd at first, but after a while I came to enjoy it. Besides, you would sound like quite the hero back in Bavaria if you said you had drunk 15 beers in an evening, all the while knowing that the equivalent volume of beer would have amounted to three mugs in the Munich beer garden!

The pubs themselves were also vastly different from the ones in Munich. Whereas in Munich the stereotype is the buxom waitress carrying several large mugs of beer in her arms, in Cologne waiters wearing blue aprons efficiently dispense the tiny glasses of beer from custom-formed serving trays. Kölsch pubs can be large, but if you are looking for the beer-hall type of setting, you're probably better off in Bavaria.

Only when I became more knowledgeable about brewing beer did I truly appreciate the skill needed to brew this crisp, refreshing golden ale that is somehow an anomaly among German beers. I discovered that Kölsch was an ale, but that it has traditionally been lagered for periods as long as eight to ten weeks to give it its smooth, mature character that makes it reminiscent of a lager. Pale, less aggressively hopped beers are among the most difficult styles to brew well, and Kölsch is certainly no exception. These noble beers don't have the assistance of specialty malts or generous additions of bittering and aroma hops to hide their imperfections. This became clear to me as a commercial brewer when I opted to sewer the first few batches of Kölsch I brewed.

Like many things in life, the deeper you go, the more interesting it gets. This certainly was the case as I began to research the history of Kölsch in preparation for writing this book. I found out that Kölsch as a beer style is actually very young, but that its roots are as old as brewing in

Germany. Indeed, Cologne has always seemed to embrace a particular style of beer at different points in time, but the clear, golden ale that Cologne is now known for has only been in existence for the last century. As I dug deeper, I learned how important the unity of the brewers of Cologne has been in making Kölsch the style that it is today and in securing its position as the only beer in the world that enjoys a protective appellation.

The citizens of Cologne must also share the same passion for Kölsch that I have. Two of every three beers drunk in Cologne is a Kölsch, and of these, one-half are consumed from the keg. In a country that is known for its beer but where overall beer production is stagnant, sales of Kölsch have actually been increasing in recent years.

Perhaps the increasing sales of Kölsch in Germany explains why it is difficult to find a bottle of German-brewed Kölsch in North America. It might be just as well, because most beers always taste better closer to the source. Whether you use this book to brew a world-class Kölsch, as a tool for planning a trip to Cologne, or as a historical point of reference, I hope you can appreciate the many levels of Kölsch as I have come to during the last 12 years. If nothing else, remember: The next time a buddy of yours tells you to try a new beer, do it! You might be pleasantly surprised to find out what you'll learn.

CHAPTER 1

The Beer
That Made
Cologne Famous

The term *Kölsch* and the beer as we know it today are actually relatively new. Kölsch as a pale, assertively hopped, top-fermented beer has only existed in the last two centuries. Even then, the Kölsch you would drink in a Cologne pub today is probably less hoppy, paler, and clearer than a Kölsch you would have drunk just 50 years ago. In fact, Kölsch has been used to describe this sparkling blonde ale only within the last 100 years. In the grand scheme of beer styles, Kölsch is actually one of the youngest in the world. One of the major reasons for this is that paler beers were generally born only in the last two centuries. The advent of the indirect fired malt kiln translated into not only beers that had less of a smoky flavor, but also beers that were paler in color. Indirect malt kilning allowed malt to be produced that was kilned not only more quickly, but also at a lower drying temperature.

This is a critical point in understanding why darker beer styles (Munich lager, stout, porter) have been around longer than pale beer styles (Kölsch, Pilsner, helles). The advent of pale malt that didn't produce smoke-flavored beer is also essential to understanding why Kölsch as we know it today probably isn't very reminiscent of the "house" beer that may have been served in Cologne 200 years ago.

What is significant about Kölsch is that it is the most recent iteration of 1,000 years of brewing tradition in Cologne. What is unique to Kölsch is that all of the brewers in Cologne, its suburbs, and adjacent towns have unified to stand behind one style of beer with relatively tightly defined parameters. Twenty-four breweries have signed the so-called Kölsch Konvention that has made Kölsch the official beer of Cologne. Can you imagine all of the brewers in San Francisco uniting and saying they will all brew California common beer? Or how about all of the brewers in Vermont stating that from this day forward they will only brew India pale ales of certain characteristics? The style parameters of Kölsch that are outlined in the Kölsch Konvention have evolved from the 1,000-year brewing tradition in Cologne, which is strongly rooted in the 700-year tradition of Cologne brewers organizing themselves to protect their rights, practice their craft, and worship God. The strong organization of Cologne's brewers has resulted in "protection" of Cologne's varying beer style(s) over the centuries. External influences—political, technological, economic, and religious—have all shaped the evolution of Cologne's beer from the early, murky brews to today's golden, sparkling Kölsch. The unusually strong bond among the brewers of Cologne over the last seven centuries has contributed immeasurably to the evolution of Cologne's beer styles and the eventual emergence of Kölsch as the one beer style on which 22 brewers are betting their futures.

The first brews of Cologne were probably variations of mead (mede, meid, meth). This beer was made by cooking grains and fermenting the juice. It was seasoned with herbs and honey. In the early Middle Ages *gruit* (*gruyt, gruth, gruyssbier*) was commonly brewed. It was made from barley or wheat, water, and different herbs. The first mention of hops being used in Cologne is in 1408. This made a dramatic improvement in the flavor and shelf life of beer. *Keutebier* (or *keute* beer) was also being brewed at the time, albeit in northern Germany. It must have been similar to Cologne's *hoppebier*, as it was made from various grains and hops. It was also known as *kewten, koite,* or *kuytbier* (Dutch). As late as 1800 there was still no mention of Kölsch as a beer style. During the Industrial Revolution in the nineteenth century, the brewers of Cologne split into two camps, the brewers of top-fermented *wiess* (not to be confused with weiss) and those who started to brew the Pilsner and export styles. During the last half of the nineteenth century, Kölsch began to surface as the name for the top-fermenting style. After World War I, Kölsch was referred to as "simple beer," probably because it was so weak due to raw-material shortages. The situation was similar after World War II, and the weak postwar brew was called "Hopfenperle." By 1950 Kölsch had established its position as the beer of Cologne and it has been gaining momentum ever since.

The Beginning of a Millennium-Long Brewing Tradition

In the ninth century there was no such thing as a commercial brewery. Brewing in Germany was done primarily by monks and "home" brewers, or estate brewers. The homebrewers were almost exclusively women, and the production of beer was for subsistence, not sale. The commercialization of brewing can be traced back to Charlemagne, the first emperor of the German Empire. Charlemagne, or Karl the Great as he was known in Germany, apparently placed great value on brewing and good beer. As his empire began to grow in the second half of the eighth century, he insisted that each of his feudal estates have a brewery (Dornbusch 1997, 26). Charlemagne provided explicit details about how the breweries should be managed, encompassing everything from quality issues to accounting procedures. Perhaps intuitively, Charlemagne understood the value of cleanliness in brewing long before eighteenth- and nineteenth-century biologists could prove it. "The administrators have to make sure that workers who use their hands in the preparation of beer, keep themselves especially clean" (Dornbusch 1997, 27).

Charlemagne understood the economic and cultural importance of beer, as well as the complexity of the brewer's craft. He even stipulated that knowledgeable tradesmen should primarily concern themselves with brewing beer (Dornbusch 1997, 27). Charlemagne's "capital" city was Aachen, a scant 40 miles from Cologne. The Emperor would travel the land to inspect his estates and monitor their productivity and quality. Thus, it is reasonable to assume that he frequented Cologne and its surrounding areas.

In the last quarter of the first millennium, monastic brewing also began to gain momentum, not just in the Rheinland area, but throughout Germany and middle Europe. At one point in the Middle Ages, it is estimated that there were more than 500 monastic breweries, with six alone in Cologne. Originally the monks brewed only for subsistence, but eventually they realized that the monastery could in part be funded through beer sales. The monks were also largely regarded as good brewers and they seemed to dedicate much effort to perfecting their brews. Eventually the monasteries started cultivating their own grain and hops, and their beer got better and stronger. Often the fathers got the strong beer, and the brothers drank the thinner beer (Sinz 1985, 23–26).

The Birth of "Kraut" Beer

The roots of Kölsch can be traced to the ninth century (Sinz 1985, 15). The evidence of the first brew made in the area near Cologne came in A.D. 873 from the Gerresheim monastery. This brew—probably a variation of mead—was certainly a far cry from the Kölsch of today and would most likely be considered undrinkable by today's standards.

Without the benefit of pasteurization, sterile filtration, or artificial preservatives, primitive brews had a very short shelf life. Whether or not the brewers knew it at the time, the herb mixtures that they added to their brews helped to lengthen the life of the medieval brews. This gruit, or *grut* (the German word for herb is *kraut*, and gruit is ye olde word for kraut) was popular until the High Middle Ages, when hops became the everyday seasoning for beer. Gruit was typically brewed using barley or wheat and then was sweetened with honey after fermentation was complete. It is difficult to imagine what gruit looked like, much less what its flavor and aroma profile was. Most likely, it was turbid and dark. It is safe to assume that the honey that was added to the gruit after fermentation affected the brew in two ways: first, it would have a lightening effect on the gruit; second, it would minimize the sour and dry edge that in all probability characterized this beer. "Primitive" beer styles that are still brewed today in Africa and Mexico are known for their sour and dry qualities. It is also more than reasonable to assume that gruit was a sour beer because of the low sanitation standards relative to today's brewing practices. Furthermore, fermentations 1,000 years ago were spontaneous, so not only yeast but also airborne bacteria were the fermentation catalysts for gruit.

It is difficult to know exactly which herbs were used and in what proportions, but in documents from the Middle Ages, references are made to oak bark, myrtle, rosemary, yarrow, and fruits from herbaceous perennials. Even as hops began to replace the herbs as the primary spice of Cologne's early brews, herbs were still often used in conjunction with the hops. Even after purity decrees that preceded the Reinheitsgebot outlawed the use of herbs, they were still employed when hop prices escalated. In the registers of Cologne from 1390 to 1400, it is noted that the flavors of ginger, anise, caraway, juniper, and gerse were very popular.

Lest anyone argue that bureaucracy is a modern development, it should be noted that the so-called *fermentarii* had full-time jobs procuring, drying, and selling the herbs. They inspected the herbs in the gruit building, where the gruit tax was also collected. Gruit was being brewed all over Germany and central Europe, and every region had its own secretive gruit herb mixes. The recipes for these herb mixes were passed down orally from one generation to the next by the fermentarii. The centuries-long tradition of gruit brewing came to a halt in 1495 after a treaty signed by Archbishop Hermann of Hessia and the City of Cologne forbade the production of it.

(An interesting anecdote about gruit brewing is that the spent grain was not eaten by livestock because they didn't like the flavors of ginger, anise, caraway, juniper, and gerse.)

Fraternities, Guilds, Corporations, and Associations

The brewers of Cologne have always been a highly organized lot. The culmination of the more than 700 years for this organization was the signing of the Kölsch Konvention in 1986, which solidified the position of Kölsch as *the* beer of Cologne and laid down its style parameters. Although the fraternities, guilds, and associations didn't explicitly dictate which types of beer the member brewers should craft, the union of the brewers in such formal organizations created the opportunity for the brewers to respond as a group and leverage their position against the government, black-market brewers, and the onslaught of foreign beers and new beer styles from other parts of Germany and the Benelux countries. This section discusses how political and commercial forces had a direct impact on the livelihood of the Cologne brewers in the Middle Ages, how the brewers responded, and, most important, how their responses affected the evolution of Cologne's indigenous beer style(s).

The estate and monastic brewers of the Middle Ages felt a common bond in their craft. Cologne brewers and monks practiced the same trade and found solace in God and their art, and unified themselves in one of the first known brewing organizations in Germany. Although official consummation didn't occur until 1396, it is assumed that the organization of Cologne's brewers was bubbling long before they formally aligned themselves.

The unification of not only the brewers, but the other trades as well, was a precursor of present-day democratic political systems and labor unions. The formation of the guilds and particularly the Brewers Guild of Cologne, the Fraternity of Saint Peter of Milano, also represented the strength of the bond that brewers both secular and monastic had with God and the Church. Additionally, by bridging the gap between monastic and secular brewing, the formation of the guilds in Cologne and all over Europe paved the way for the birth of commerce and free trade as we know it.

Why was the brewers guild called the Fraternity of Saint Peter of Milano? It was common for the guilds or trades to choose a patron saint, and the monks and the brewers of Cologne chose the Dominican Saint Peter of Milano. The Dominicans first came to Cologne in 1221. Their monastery, the Holy Cross, is first mentioned in 1233. (Famous holy men such as Antonius Senesis and Thomas Aquinas both stayed and taught at this monastery and church.) Peter of Milano fought hard for the true religion and unity of the Church. He was murdered in 1252, and his death was mourned throughout the Christian world. One year after his death, Innocent IV declared him a saint (Mathar/Spiegel 1989, 21).

The significance and pervasiveness of Christianity in daily life in thirteenth-century Cologne is akin to the impact that microprocessors have in developed nations today. Just as few people go through a day in the United States without their lives being affected by microprocessors, very few middle Europeans in the Middle Ages were not influenced by the Christian vision of God. Brewers, both monastic and secular, were no exception. Both always prayed to God that their brews would be successful. The theory at the time was that the brew would only be a success if it was blessed by God. Before the advent of refrigeration, microscopes, and pure culture yeast, many brews would turn sour. While working, brewers sang religious songs, surmising that the beer would flourish if prepared in

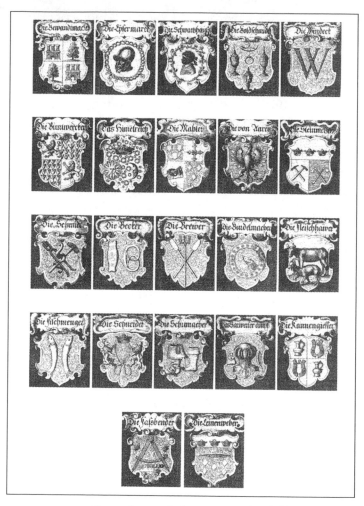

*Coat of arms belonging to the different trades
that joined the Guild Alliance of Cologne.*

a festive setting. If many bad batches did occur, the brewers would try to keep the evil spirits away by using herbs (à la garlic and vampires!) or by blocking the door to the fermentation rooms with giant beams.

The heathens of an earlier period were also superstitious. A common custom of Germanic origin was to dribble freshly brewed beer on the ground, thus calling up earth spirits while drinking (Sinz 1985, 27). The importance of religion at the time is underscored by the fact that all important guild affairs were started with a religious service. This included the so-called master's feast, as well as guild elections and the acceptance of journeymen.

A struggle against archbishops and feudal lords that had lasted for at least two centuries peaked when the tradesmen of Cologne banded together in 1396 to sign a letter of alliance. It unified them under a new guild system that addressed their political and economic needs. All told, 22 different trades came together to form the Guild Alliance of Cologne. The variety of trades and professions that joined is extremely interesting: four different groups of knights, tanners, weavers, gold smiths, glass blowers, bakers, butchers, coopers, shoemakers, and, of course, brewers (see illustration opposite this page).

The roots of the guilds in Cologne go back to 1149, when authorities confirmed the textile makers' guild. All tradesmen were forced to join their respective guilds. The functions of the guilds were many, and they included monitoring trade and methods of production, educating apprentices, establishing rules of trade and commerce, defining criteria for membership, collecting entry fees and dues, setting wage standards, and determining where and when to sell products.

Although the guilds ultimately served the interests of their members, they were bureaucratic and derived much of their revenue from that membership. Everything was very clearly laid out in the covenants of the guild. For example, the covenants dictated how each finger was to be held during the swearing of an oath and explained the religious symbolism of each finger. The thumb meant God the Father, and the pointer finger meant the Holy Spirit. From old guild books it is also known what the prices were for each individual oath. The new official master Engel Hoekkeshouen swore his oath before the fraternity in 1589. He had to pay four gold gulden for this. If one considers that on average a tradesman earned 35 gulden in a year, this is quite a nice "processing fee" (Mathar/Spiegel 1989, 22).

The guilds often served the interests of the community as well and were always prepared to serve the citizens of Cologne. Whether the poor or indigent were in need of assistance or a fire needed to be fought, the members of the brewers guild were there to assist. Members of guilds even functioned as a citizens' militia (Sinz 1985, 27–38).

Brewers typically had a four-year apprenticeship and then spent two years as journeymen before they could become independent. To do that, they had to pass a test and pay fees. Then a master's feast was given. Once an individual became an independent brewmaster, the choices were to inherit, buy, or rent a brewery. Interestingly, the right to brew stayed with the brewery. Occasionally, the city allowed a new brewery to be built, but the right to brew remained with the building. This was largely a means of protection against foreign competition (Sinz 1985, 31).

The guild liked it if the brewmaster was married to a "Cologne daughter of Catholic parents." In that case the guild would even chip in to help defray the cost of the master's feast. A typical feast included 40 pounds of fresh ox meat, 24 pounds of smoked ox meat, 24 pounds of ham, 40 pounds of veal, and 16 pounds of Dutch cheese. All of this was to feed 100 to 120 people. Of course, there were also unlimited quantities of beer, and other things to eat, such as chicken, lamb, sausage, rabbit, other game, cakes, apples, pears, and nuts (Sinz 1985, 32–33).

The formation of guilds in Cologne, and in particular the founding of the Fraternity of Saint Peter of Milano as the binding organization for Cologne's brewers, represented the transition from feudal estate brewing and monastic brewing to commercial brewing. This sociopolitical revolution created a platform for commercial brewers to gain control of their destiny. The founding of the guilds and fraternities did not end the brewers' struggles against political and economic forces, but it did create a position of strength that the brewers used to determine the history of brewing in Cologne, and the continued evolution of Cologne's medieval brews into the Kölsch of today.

The Middle Ages, the Patron Saint of Brewers, and the New Beer in Town

To many brewers, he is known as *the* patron saint of brewing. To the residents of Cologne, he is one of the biggest heroes in the city's history. Gambrinus and Jan Primus (also known as Jan I, *primus* being Latin for "the first") of Brabant are one and the same. Jan Primus was instrumental in winning the Battle of Worringen in 1288. Together with the Dukes of Looz and Jülich as well as the residents of Cologne, Jan Primus defeated the Archbishop of Cologne and the Dukes of Luxembourg and Gelder. The victory was significant not only for the residents of Cologne but for the guilds as well, as they wrested power from the Church and took over rule of the city. The city of Cologne thought so highly of Jan's

contribution in the battle that it made him an honorary citizen and built him a house within the city walls.

Jan Primus (Gambrinus) was a legendary warrior and knight and was also given honorary membership in the Brewers Guild of Brussels for his bravery. He most likely became known as the king, inventor, and patron saint of beer through a printing or

interpretation mistake made in a sixteenth-century verse, in which Gambrinus was fully and arbitrarily connected to brewers. The legend was supported by a painting from 1526 in which Jan Primus is depicted with stalks of barley in his crown. This now famous painting belongs to the Bavarian Brewers Association and is hanging in the German Brewery Museum in Munich.

The Battle of Worringen was the climax of a decades-long struggle among the emerging tradesmen (including brewers), the Church, and the feudal lords. Cologne was no exception to the rest of Germany in the continuous struggle among the state, the Church, and the private sector to establish brewing rights. This struggle went on for the better part of 1,000 years, and it was clearly a strong impetus toward the formation of brewers guilds, unions, and other associations. Organization and unification is more likely to occur in times of strife than peace, and the fact that brewers constantly had their brewing rights granted and rescinded by various authorities certainly led to the development of a common cause.

It's no surprise that this struggle was centered on taxation issues. By the year 1212 brewers were triple taxed: (1) on the grain they used to make beer with, (2) on the brewing vessels and vats, and (3) on the final product. While the city of Cologne was making out handsomely at the expense of the brewers, the Church realized it was missing out on a large source of revenue. Whereas in 1212 the city council of Cologne had persuaded Emperor Otto IV to let them tax the brewers, Archbishop Conrad of Hochstaden convinced the succeeding emperor, Frederick II, to let the Church collect the taxes again. The city council was none too pleased, so the whole issue went into arbitration. In the end, the Dominican monk, Albertus Magnus, pronounced that the city and the Church would each collect half of the taxes (Dornbusch 1997, 54–55).

Of course, this decision really didn't benefit the brewers or the beer drinkers. The brewers tried to circumvent the malt tax by simply brewing thinner beer. The "powers that be" didn't realize that the oppressive taxation served to help the brewers organize and thereby gain political momentum. This is a prime example of how the organized brewers responded to political impulses and how their response affected the style of beer brewed in Cologne at the time. Whether the masses enjoyed this thin version of gruit is unknown, but it is interesting that the gruit brewed at the time apparently became thinner across the board.

Around 1400, another occurrence had a significant impact on what type of beer was brewed in Cologne, and both the guild's and city council's reactions were instrumental in the continued evolution of Cologne's beer toward Kölsch. So-called keutebier came to Cologne from northern Germany. As was previously mentioned, thinner, gruit-style beer had become somewhat of a standard in Cologne, as the brewers attempted to circumvent the malt tax. There is evidence that guild members in Cologne were brewing some beer that contained hops, but keutebier, made from malt and hops, was a thicker, heavier beer, and gained popularity in Cologne to the point where it affected the local brewers (Mathar/Spiegel 1989, 12). The local brewers who did choose to use hops did so for three reasons: (1) it imparted an enjoyable flavor to the beer; (2) it increased the stability of beer; and (3) hops were not taxed at the time, so it was less expensive to use hops than gruit. In the mid-1400s, keutebier brewers were not allowed in the guild.

The city council finally had to allow the brewers more freedom to compete against the importation of the keute beer (and shore up the lost tax revenue). The guild also recognized the keute beer brewers and allowed them into the guild in 1471. Of course, this compromise was accompanied by a modification of use taxes to include hops! By that time there were almost 60 members in the guild, with 41 keute or hop-beer brewers and only 18 thin-beer brewers in Cologne (Sinz 1985, 23; Mathar/Spiegel 1989, 12).

By 1495 gruit beer brewing became illegal in Cologne. This was concurrent with more widespread, feudal and governmental mandates in Germany to change from using unmalted grains, honey, and herbs to brew "beer" to using only certain grains and hops. We need look no further than the Bavarian Purity Law of 1516 to see this, as it mentions only barley, hops, and water. At that time there was still no concept of pure culture yeast used to control fermentation and, ultimately, beer flavor.

The exact reasons why the numerous purity laws were decreed throughout Germany varied, but the issuance of these decrees usually centered around taxation. Historians generally accept that gruit-style beers were of such varying quality that drinkers were consuming less of these poor-tasting beers. In an effort to keep beer consumption, and subsequently tax revenue, from falling, these purity decrees were handed down all over Germany in the twelfth to sixteenth centuries in one form or another. It also stands to reason that simplifying the choice of ingredients also made it easier for the "bad guys" to manage ingredient/use taxes as well.

The city and the brewers were constantly at odds over issues surrounding taxation. In 1555 the city council took over the brewers' monopoly and brewing became highly regulated and centralized. Citizen brewers were forced to brew in city-owned breweries under the strict supervision of two brewmasters. Guild membership dropped from 89 in 1500 to 60 or 70 by the late 1500s. In 1603 the city further attempted to strengthen its position by mandating that only top-fermented beer could be brewed in Cologne. Naturally, the bureaucrats hadn't learned anything before, so in 1607, under the pressure of declining beer sales (i.e., decreasing tax revenue), the city decentralized brewing and leased the rights to brew back to the brewers. Guild membership consequently rose to 90, and by the end of the Middle Ages there were approximately 100 breweries in Cologne (Mathar/Spiegel 1989, 12–13).

In the late Middle Ages lager brewing appeared, but it never really took hold in Cologne. Cologne has a more temperate climate than the Alps region where lager brewing took off. Only in the coldest conditions can beer age over many weeks. In warmer climates beer that was lagered went sour quickly. (As noted previously, the city council of Cologne even forbade lager brewing.) Often Kölsch had an acidic note during the warmer months, and

---

BREWERS IN COLOGNE in the Middle Ages lived reasonably well. Many brewers actually lived in homes or buildings, in contrast to most of the citizens of Cologne, who lived in individual rooms. Often the brewers, apprentices, and journeymen lived in the brewery building, a tradition that continues today in Germany. In exchange for this relatively good standard of living, the medieval brewer put in long days, usually 12 to 16 hours. It is true that in Cologne in 1400 there were 110 Sundays and holidays, but that just meant more free time for the masses to drink beer. The brewers had to work even harder to keep up with the demand created by idle time (Sinz 1985, 50).

---

if it was sour, then the batch was dumped. Because beers brewed during the winter months were much less likely to go bad, the price of a beer was less between October and April (Sinz 1985, 52–53). The drinkers of Cologne were a tough crowd, and batches or brands they didn't like were given names such as "Murder and Death," "Cow Mouth," "Crawling on the Wall," "Gutrot," and "Bitchy Maid" (Sinz 1985, 53).

A spin-off of the heavy taxation and regulation of the brewing industry in Cologne was the development of a black market for beer. There were many "hacker" brewers, who basically brewed out of their basements and sold beer on the black market. Although homebrewing for personal consumption was legal, the city council tried to limit the hackers by saying they could only brew once a year. Many of these hackers would set up shop just outside the Cologne city limits and then sell their black market brew (Sinz 1985, 39–40).

Cologne in the Middle Ages was very bureaucratic and "rule happy." The city council of Cologne concerned itself with many things in addition to the administration of brewing, such as the number of guests allowed at a wedding reception and how people could dress. Fasching has always been a huge event in Cologne, but in some years masquerading was forbidden because the city was afraid there would be too much "nonsense." It is still customary to dress in costume for some of the big days, such as Fat Tuesday (Sinz 1985, 51).

The brewers of Cologne also produced malt mostly for their own use, but many also gave or sold their excess to small, country breweries or homebrewers. The local authorities constantly tried to tax this malt production. In the thirteenth, fourteenth, and fifteenth centuries there were open malt sales in the center of town. One brewery still makes its home at the location of the malt market and is appropriately named Malzmühle (malt mill). This malt mill was located near a stream, and apparently things got a little testy when farmers would divert the flow of water away from the malt mill's paddlewheel (Sinz 1985, 54–56). Distilling also gained in popularity during the Middle Ages, and from 1500 to 1800 the number of distilleries increased to 90. Although the distillers stayed out of the brewers guilds, they didn't form their own guild.

By the end of the Middle Ages the type of beer that was brewed in Cologne had undergone a major transformation. At the center of this change was the brewers guild and the Fraternity of Saint Peter of Milano. The guild responded to oppressive taxation by brewing a thinner version of gruit to circumvent taxation based on strength. As the new style of beer, keutebier, became popular in Cologne, the guild responded by allowing keutebier brewers into the guild. This change paralleled a more widespread revolution in Germany that forever suppressed gruit-style brewing and firmly secured the place of hops in beer. Honey and herbs were out; hops and barley were in.

The End of the Guilds and the Beginnings of Pale Beers

In 1794 the French occupied Cologne, and in 1797 they declared free trade and dissolved not only the brewers guild, but all guilds for all trades. The Fraternity of Saint Peter of Milano remained as the only trade organization of Cologne, renaming itself Colner Brauer Corporation, or Corporation of Cologne Brewers. With the French occupation and the elimination of the fraternities and guilds, "organized labor" took on new meaning. The biggest change brought about by French-imposed free trade was the diminishing impact religion and the Church had on guilds and unions. A huge shift occurred as the commercial importance of organized labor supplanted the spiritual bond tradesmen and guilds had with God and the Church.

By 1815 the French were out, Napoleon was on his way to exile, and the Prussians took over. It wasn't until 1845 that the guilds and fraternities became legal again. The guild-free years made the resurrected guilds more social than political organizations. Without the protection of the guild, less friendly competition intensified. More important, the guild-free era in Cologne and the less political nature of the resurrected guilds after 1845 signified a less-organized epoch for the brewers of Cologne. This lack of organization undoubtedly contributed to the subsequent diversification of beer styles in Cologne in the nineteenth and early twentieth centuries.

As the urbanization of Cologne and its suburbs progressed, so did the growth of the larger breweries. By 1900 there were only 60 top-fermenting breweries left in Cologne, down from a high of 119 in 1861. The larger breweries were mainly producers of lagers, which were more stable than the top-fermented beer from the small breweries. These small breweries generally served their beer on their premises and in neighboring pubs, whereas the larger breweries had a vaster distribution radius, and many exported their beer to nearby Holland and Belgium (Sinz 1985, 60–61).

ALTHOUGH THE GUILDS had lost much of their importance and functionality during the nineteenth century, one of the strongest trade organizations ever formed in Germany was about to make its debut. In July 1871, shortly after the end of the Franco-Prussian War, more than 1,000 German brewers gathered in Dresden to celebrate the founding of the German Brewers Association. This unification of the brewers of Germany was somehow symbolic of the greater German political unification that was occurring simultaneously. Just as the many previous attempts at political unification in Germany had failed in the past, the German brewers had been unable to unite in the 1850s because of the variations in the beer tax laws from state to state. The event was well attended by brewers all over Europe and from as far away as America.

The association created a great opportunity for German brewers to discuss the technological advances in brewing, resulting from the Industrial Revolution. Through the years, the association had many functions, one of the more notable was to provide the troops in World War I with beer. The Nazis dissolved the German Brewers Association in 1934. The association wasn't able to regroup immediately after the World War II because the marshal law imposed by the Allies at the end of the war forbade all organizations. By April 1, 1949, however, the German Brewers Association was formally allowed to reconvene, which it did in Frankfurt (Sinz 1985, 95–97).

In 1890 the number of pubs that could open was limited by law, and hours of operation were also shortened. This benefited the Cologne's small brewers, who had a well-defined number of local and loyal customers. In the early 1900s bottling helped the large and small brewers sell more product. As a result, by 1913 there were more than 100 beer distributors in Cologne, and per capita consumption in Cologne had risen to 154 liters.

From the late nineteenth century through the early 1930s, many "brewers organizations" were simply unions. As centuries of the patriarchal relationship

between owners and workers came to an end, these organizations brought to the forefront one of the most critical questions involving brewing: what are the rights of the twentieth-century brewer? The difference between these unions and the guilds or associations wasn't always black and white, but essentially a union could only look after its members from a labor standpoint, not having a market-regulating or sociopolitical function (Sinz 1985, 98–99).

As the guilds were fading into insignificance, technological advances resulting from the Industrial Revolution were accelerating and having an enormous impact on the development of beer production, flavor, and stability. No other century has had as great an impact on the development and evolution of beer styles worldwide as the nineteenth. In those 100 years, technological developments changed beer forever: refrigeration, filtration, single-cell propagations of yeast, the invention of the bottle cap, and bottling of beer are just a few. What perhaps had the greatest impact on the evolution of beer styles was the invention of the indirect heated kiln. The first implementation of this new method of kilning occurred in 1818, and from that day forward darker, smokier-flavored beers have been losing market share (Dornbusch 1997, 80). The new hot-air kiln replaced the old method of using flue gases to dry and kiln malt, which made them smoke flavored and usually darker.

To appreciate why this was the case, think of cooking over an open fire versus baking in a convection oven. To cook something thoroughly over an open fire without burning it generally means it needs to be a fair distance from the hot part of the fire. This "slow cooking" is exactly how dark malt is made because if the malt is too close to the open fire, it will burn. The "lower and slower" method

The Nineteenth-Century Pub in Cologne

A VISIT TO A nineteenth-century pub in Cologne would be an interesting experience, indeed. Let's go back in time 150 years and experience it for ourselves! As we approach the pub, we notice a smoldering brick of tanbark next to the entrance in an iron basket, with which we can use to light a pipe or warm our hands. Entering the pub, we notice a willow basket filled with hops hanging from the entrance to the pub and we have to push aside the hop vines.

Once inside the pub, we find ourselves in a hallway entrance where we would stay to order a quick beer. This also serves as the location where hangmen, knackers, and executioners drink their beer from broken mugs without lids. But we are destined for the heart of the pub, so we further our way. (The egalité of the French Revolution nominally brought this to an end, but even then, as Ernst Weyden observed, the hallway was still always reserved for "certain classes" [Mathar/Spiegel 1989, 119–21].)

Our typical pub has oak wainscot and oak tables and benches. An uncertain "light-darkness" (*weyden*) is present. The smoke from the iron tallow lanterns competes against the heavy fog of tobacco smoke.

Pipe smoking is quite stylish, and the typical clay pipe is called a "nosewarmer." Racks on the wall hold long, earthen pipes. Finer people have brought their own Meerschaum pipes in leather or silk cases. Tobacco is provided in the pub and lays on the table. Some patrons are even smoking pipes with bowls made out of gypsum that have been soaked in linseed oil. The stench emanating from these particular pipes is awful.

Our main objective at hand is, of course, to drink beer. There are several types of beer available for us to choose from, depending on the time of year. Märzer (note the difference here between the Märzer and Bavarian Märzen, which is brewed in the spring for consumption in the fall) is a spring beer; alt and *steckenalt* are customary in summer; and in the fall and winter pub goers enjoy *knupp, jungbier* (green beer, as in not fully aged), or *halv und halv* (a precursor to today's black and tan?).

Our fine offerings are customarily served in clay mugs with pewter lids. The walls of the pub are lined with these mugs. Glassware is uncommon, and only the rich can afford this luxury. The pub doesn't stock the glassware, but look, there comes a patron with a braided willow basket. Nestled in the basket is his glass.

A testament to the quality and consistency of the beer of the time (or lack thereof) seems to be the fact that most guests are carrying a chunk of nutmeg and a grater to rub a little spice into their beer. Many are adding a slice of lemon to their beer, also a common practice.

Most of the pub's business is in the evening, and playing cards appears to be a very popular pastime. The *stammtisch* is occupied by the well-to-do citizens, who are deemed worthy enough to sit at this table. The intellectuals and professionals (painters, lithographers, editors, and authors) usually frequent the wine houses. (Around the turn of the century these types began to appear at the brew houses and the stammtisch became a magnet for all types of beer lovers, not just the elite. [Mathar/Spiegel 1989, 119–23].)

used to wither dark malt is what develops the sugars and protein substances that produce the dark colors and malty flavors in the hot part of the final phase of kilning. The convection oven allows the product being cooked to be brought to high temperatures quickly without "scorching" effects. This is the exact process used to make pale malt. In other words, dark malts are produced by "stewing" the green malt for as long as 24 hours at lower temperatures and then kilning at high temperatures. Pale malts are made by stewing, or withering, at higher temperatures for shorter periods of time, but then kilning at lower temperatures than are used to produce dark malt. It is difficult to make a pale malt with a direct fired kiln because it is tricky to achieve the high withering temperature without scorching the grain, and it is just as cumbersome to kiln the malt at lower temperatures and still get the grain hot enough so it will dry.

The effect of the indirect malt kiln on Cologne's beer led to the birth of the first cousin of Kölsch. This beer was still not completely like today's Kölsch, but the *altrheinisches-hopfenbitteres lagerbier* shares some common traits with Kölsch. This beer is actually referred to as "Alt," but it should not be confused with the darker version that is still served 40 kilometers down the river in Düsseldorf. A thorough description of the hop-bitter lager beer follows in subsequent chapters, but in a German book published in 1938, this beer is described as "having been in existence for more than 100 years, golden-yellow in color, highly hopped, and having a starting gravity of 8 to 9 °Plato" (Schönfeld 1938, 164–65). This beer was also referred to as Kölsch wiess, but was not yet the recent version of Kölsch due to the style differences just outlined and because it was unfiltered. This beer was one of the main beer styles in Cologne during the eighteenth and early nineteenth centuries. Of course, the development of the indirect, hot-air kiln also led to the development of what is the most popular beer style in the world today: Pilsner. As was mentioned earlier, pale lagers also made their presence known in and around Cologne.

By the beginning of the twentieth century, the impact that the organization of Cologne's brewers had on the city's beer styles was clear. It was minimal, precisely because the sociopolitical climate at the time was not conducive to the brewers being organized, thus directing the evolution of keutebier into the new beer of Cologne. The dissolution of the guilds, the Industrial Revolution, the acceleration of capitalism and free market economies, and specific technological changes that affected beer production and quality all fostered diversity of beer styles not only in Cologne, but all over Germany. Furthermore, the changes resulted in a gradual transformation from brewpubs to full-scale breweries that kegged and bottled beer for sale at locations away from the on-site brewery outlet. Appendix A will make clear just how many breweries were part of this evolution and how diverse Cologne's beer styles were in the first half of the twentieth century. Unfortunately, it took two world wars and an economic crisis to reunite Cologne's brewers and produce what unequivocally became Cologne's one and only beer style.

Kölsch Becomes Kölsch

The social and economic impacts the two world wars had on Germany are well known. But how did these wars affect the brewers of Germany and, in particular, Cologne and its beer? The common thread between both was that as the wars went on, the beer got weaker. Rationing in 1915 allowed brewers to use only 60% of the malt they normally used. By 1917 this level was down to 10%. Rationing naturally translated into a large reduction in the production of beer from the breweries. Before the war, German breweries processed 1.2 million metric tons of barley. By the end of the war, the brewers received only 120,000 tons. The gravities of the beers sank to extremely low levels. Brewers were ashamed, but the people had the right attitude: it was better than nothing.

Delivery trucks came on the scene just before World War I. The purchase of these beer delivery trucks was often subsidized, but with the condition that the trucks had to be available to the military if needed during war. Another interesting development during both of the world wars was that women came back into the *brauhaus* after a centuries-long hiatus (Sinz 1985, 79–81). After World War I, beer consumption in Germany dropped to half of prewar levels (Mathar/Spiegel 1989, 13).

By the end of World War I, the term *Kölsch* was used by at least one brewery to describe the regional specialty beer that was the hop-bitter lager beer. The more common specialties of the region, which also included Düsseldorf, were the hop-bitter lager beer/wiess, alt, and steckenalt. In the 1920s the distinction was first made between *echt* Kölsch, which was filtered, and Kölsch wiess, which was not. Beer filtration did not become prevalent until the turn of the century, and echt Kölsch was simply a filtered version of wiess. It can't be emphasized enough that during the late nineteenth century and first half of the twentieth century, brewers in Cologne were embracing the bottom-fermented lager styles in much the same way that the rest of Central Europe was.

(The best analogy that I can draw to this phenomenon would be the advent of the specialty-beer revolution in North America that began in the 1980s.) The new lager styles were exactly that: new. These styles forever changed the landscape of beer styles in Germany. Many of Cologne's breweries were brewing the regional specialty products, but no single style really emerged as the front-runner. The traditional Kölsch wiess/hop-bitter lager beer was popular in Cologne, but it wasn't until after World War II that Kölsch emerged as the dominant beer style in Cologne. The breweries' descriptions in appendix A provides more insight into the diversity of beer styles in Cologne during this period.

The 1930s were particularly hard for the brewers of Cologne and all of Germany. In 1930 the excise tax on beer was raised 46%. In 1932 the price commissioner ordered a 2.25 Mark reduction in the price brewers could charge for their beer! Of course, this brilliant idea had no real chance of increasing beer sales because rampant unemployment in Germany at the time meant there was less disposable income for such purchases. All of this led to intensely brutal competition among the brewers. Brewing guilds and organizations tried stepping in to mitigate the battle, but for most of the breweries it was an issue of survival (Sinz 1985, 91–93).

With the advent of the Third Reich, the economic conditions in Germany improved, as did the environment for the breweries. Even at the beginning of World War II, beer production was still high, as beer was being shipped to the troops in the countries Germany occupied. One of the problems Cologne faced in the second war that it had not in the first was intense air bombing. There were 262 air raids on Cologne during World War II. This resulted in a large number of interruptions in operations at breweries throughout the city.

The extent of the damage Cologne endured during the Second World War is mind boggling. The air attacks from 1942 to 1945 cost many Cologners their lives and destroyed 90% of the inner city of Cologne. Literally hundreds of thousands of inhabitants had to leave the city after their homes were destroyed. By the end of the war, the city that once boasted 750,000 residents was down to 40,000, and the city center was a completely bombed out ghost town (Mathar/Spiegel 1989, 113). Somehow the cathedral in Cologne managed to come out of the war intact. Visitors to Cologne today should note that structures surrounding the cathedral are of postwar construction.

During the first large air attack on May 30, 1942 (the so-called thousand-bomb attack), the breweries Dom, Sion, and Unter Taschenmacher were wiped out. A particularly

resilient brewery was the Früh am Hof brewery. Bombed twice during air attacks, the occupying British troops finally brought it to its knees when they torched it in 1945. After 505 years, the number of breweries in Cologne was back down to 21. By the end of the war, there were only two operating breweries. All of the other brew houses in the city were burned out, their tanks riddled with bullet holes, and their cellars rendered useless.

As was the case during World War I, beer became quite thin and bland. I have personally heard stories of wartime beer having a starting gravity as low as 1.5 °Plato, compared to today's starting gravities of 11 to 12.5 °Plato. To at least give the beer some type of hue, sugar coloring was allowed. This, of course, was in strong contravention with the Reinheitsgebot.

Even the production of these thin beers became difficult as the war progressed. If breweries weren't completely destroyed, they had difficulty obtaining spare parts. The supply of electricity and fossil fuels needed for brewing also became scarcer as the war drew to a close. As if that wasn't enough, all of the qualified brewers were either drafted or killed during bomb attacks.

After the war, the brew kettles in Cologne were slowly fired up again. Brewing became quite an adventure because raw materials often had to be smuggled past occupying troops. Kegs of beer were often transported in ambulances to avoid confiscation. Luckily, the British troops occupying the Cologne area were beer lovers, so it was also in their interest to see that the breweries resumed production as soon as possible. For the drinker who just had to have a full-strength beer, there was always the black market, but the price was outrageous. By 1946 there were three breweries producing beer, and by 1947 the count was up to 13.

The Kölsch Konvention

It took the complete destruction of a city and its breweries for Cologne to once again unify itself under one dominant beer style: Kölsch. There is no explanation in any of the material I came across when writing this book as to why Kölsch became the dominant beer style in and around Cologne. (Appendix A makes clear that after World War II most of Cologne's breweries began narrowing their selection of products down to this one style.) All we can surmise is that the complete destruction of the city and its brewing tradition somehow unified its brewers in a way that led them back to their roots. Cologne has always had a strong sense of identity and independence, and possibly the adversity suffered by all during and after the war led the brewers to rally around the traditional style as a way to reaffirm the city's rich tradition.

Perhaps the founding of the Association of Cologne Breweries after the war led to more than just unification of producers. This organization exists alongside the Cologne Brewers Corporation, but it has assumed the duty of protecting and promoting Kölsch in modern times. In this highly competitive and litigious era of free commerce that we now live in, it is truly remarkable that a group of industry leaders could band together to protect their product and their livelihood from competing companies. The so-called Kölsch Konvention, or Kölsch pact, is recognized by the German government and gives the 22 participating breweries in and around Cologne the exclusive right to call their beer Kölsch. When the Kölsch brewers met in 1986 to sign the historic document, they realized that "the Konvention marked an end of a decades long discussion that centered around the question of whether Kölsch was simply a style description or also one of origin" (Mathar/Spiegel 1989, 146).

This appellation—similar to Scotch whisky, champagne, and chianti—protects the producers within the geographic region from the onslaught of wanna-be producers. The producers who enjoy the protection of the geographically based appellation argue that the consumer is protected from bogus products. In the case of Kölsch, the purchaser of a glass or bottle of this style can be sure that he or she is purchasing the real goods, which has been brewed within the greater Cologne area.

The Kölsch Konvention goes beyond just the simple protection of the appellation. The signatories of the Konvention agreed that descriptors such as "true," "original," "special," or "premium" are not allowed. To

guarantee the geographic purity of Kölsch, it was also agreed that any contract-brewed Kölsch has to be produced at a brewery within the Kölsch region. Finally, there are even specifications regarding the labeling of kegs and Kölsch glasses. Violators of the competitive rules of the pact can be fined up to 250,000 German Marks and/or be banned from the Cologne Brewers Association.

What is the motivation for the Kölsch Konvention? In a country dominated by the Pilsner style, why be concerned about protecting a relatively obscure beer style? It is exactly because of its obscurity that the 22 member breweries of the Cologne Brewery Association signed the pact. They don't want Kölsch to experience the same fate that Pilsner did. Not only American light beers, but also any old swill produced in tropical countries, is called Pilsner, and the Kölsch brewers didn't want to see their beer style diluted as Pilsner has been. The anniversary of the signing of the Kölsch Konvention is celebrated every year in Cologne and is well attended by the member brewers as well as local and national dignitaries.

Today Kölsch is strengthening its position in the otherwise contracting German beer market, but the picture has not necessarily been rosy for all of Cologne's brewers.

The mega beverage conglomerate Brau & Brunnen (which is the parent company of Germany Brewery Holding) owns one-third of the Kölsch brands. Many brands are also contract brewed, or their brand prestige has been eroded to the point where they are only available as discount beers in large chain stores.

In Cologne today there is a full spectrum of producers who are all bound together by one style. As in the American beer market, there are small brewpubs, medium-sized family breweries, contract-brewed Kölsch brands, and a few giants. Through the first nine months of 1997, production among Kölsch brewers was actually up 0.5%, while the production of the total number from breweries in the North Rhine-Westphalia province was down 1.6%. The production of *altbier* in nearby Düsseldorf shrank by 4% in this period. More than half of all Kölsch produced ends up in a keg—a testament to the conviction of the Kölsch drinkers and their commitment to their beer. In a time when the large breweries in Germany are sucking away market share from local producers, the citizens of Cologne continue to support the brewing tradition that makes their city one of the truly great brewing centers of the world.

Like so many things in life, the story of Kölsch has somehow come full circle. From the murky, primitive gruit beers, to the trendy and revolutionary keutebier and lager styles, it is now Kölsch that is the style that has unified the brewers of Cologne. More likely, it is the unification of the brewers of Cologne that has resulted in Kölsch becoming the dominant style in a city that has outlasted entire civilizations. Whether or not Kölsch will be the dominant style in Cologne in 100 years is anybody's guess. If history does repeat itself, there will probably be a period in the future in which there is once again style diversity and fragmentation in Cologne, followed by a paring down of styles. For now, none of that matters. What is important is to salute the brewers of Cologne, their perseverance, their unification, and their unique and wonderful beer that belongs only to them.

CHAPTER 2

Sensory Profile and Chemical Composition

Unlike some beer styles such as stout, weissbier, or Scotch ale, Kölsch is a fairly "tight" style in terms of original gravity (OG), color, and carbonation. There is some variation in pH and bitterness, but the senses have to be well tuned to appreciate the subtle differences among Kölsch brands. The commonalities among Kölsch are fairly unifying:

- Kölsch is golden in color, typically in the range of 7 to 14 EBC units (3.5 to 7 SRM units);
- Kölsch is top fermented (i.e., ale);

- Kölsch is generally filtered until its clear;
- Kölsch is highly attenuated, giving it a refreshing and tangy character;
- Kölsch typically has a starting gravity of 11 to 14 °Plato (there are some examples of "light" Kölsch and alcohol-free Kölsch in the market), but most have an OG of 11 to 12.5 °Plato;
- Kölsch is moderately hopped with German hops, typically in the range of 16 to 34 IBUs.

These general similarities do not mean that a Kölsch is a Kölsch is a Kölsch. Differences in yeast and yeast management, water, malt, hops, and brewing practices among the Kölsch breweries all add up to variations in flavor, aroma, carbonation, mouthfeel, and chemical composition.

Original Gravity and Alcohol

If you're looking for a big, high-alcohol beer, you should probably bypass Cologne and head to Bavaria for some *doppelbock*. Kölsch has typically been a low-gravity, low-alcohol beer. In fact, the starting gravities of Kölsch used to be 8 to 9 °Plato before the Biersteuergesetz, or the beer tax law, was adopted in 1906 in Bismarck's Germany. Many confuse the Reinheitsgebot with the Biersteuergesetz. The Reinheitsgebot is the anchor or fundamental philosophy behind the Biersteuergesetz and is actually part of the tax law, but it is the Biersteuergesetz that regulates everything from how a beer can be carbonated to what starting gravity a German beer is allowed to have.

The Biersteuergesetz created original-gravity classes that include all beers brewed in Germany. Normal or *vollhier* is 11 to 14 °Plato, *bock* beer is above 16, and the original gravity of so-called *schank,* or light beer, is between 7 and 8 °Plato. Beers with starting gravities between these categories are called "gap" beers and until recently were illegal to brew. With the advent of the Biersteuergesetz in 1906, the starting gravities of Kölsch went up from 8 to 9 °Plato to the 11 to 12 °Plato range.

Today most examples of Kölsch are brewed with an original gravity between 11 and 12 °Plato, with most falling in the fat part of the bell curve at 11.2 to 11.8 °Plato. Most German Pilsners and American-style lagers fall in this same range. Table 1 shows how the original gravities of Kölsch compare to each other and to a couple of other styles.

TABLE 1

Comparison of Original Gravity (OG), Apparent Degree of Attenuation, Apparent Terminal Gravity, and Alcohol by Volume (ABV) among Different Kölsch Beers, and Closely Related German and American Styles

Beer Brand or Style[a]	OG (°Plato)	Apparent Degree of Attenuation	Apparent Terminal Gravity	ABV (%)
Kölsch #1	11.6	83.8	1.88	
Kölsch #2	11.4	82.0	2.05	
Kölsch #3	11.5	81.7	2.10	
Kölsch #4	11.8	83.8	1.91	
Kölsch #5	11.3	79.9	2.27	
Kölsch #6	12.0	85.5	1.74	
Kölsch #7	11.27	83.9	1.81	5.0
Kölsch light	7.4	67.0	2.44	2.5
German Pilsner	11.2–12.5		3.5–5.0	4.0–5.0
Bavarian helles	11.0–13.0		2.0–3.0	4.5–5.5
American lager	11.0–13.0		1.5–2.5	4.0–4.5

[a]Information on beers 1 to 6, which are commercial examples, are from lecture notes of a presentation by Ludwig Narziss; information for Kölsch #7 is provided by a brewery; information on German Pilsner, Bavarian helles, and American lager is from the *North American Brewers Resource Directory* (Boulder, Colo.: Brewers Publications, 1997).

The alcohol content of Kölsch is high relative to the starting gravity due to the high degree of attenuation.

Most Kölsch beers have an alcohol content of 4.5 to 5.2% by volume. This table shows how highly attenuated Kölsch is as a style. Only light lagers, dry beers, and German dietetic beers have attenuation degrees that are as high or higher.

Leveraging off the tremendous popularity of light beers in America, German brewers began brewing light beers in the 1980s, thinking that these products would be the new big trend. In contrast to American light beers,* the intent behind the German light beers was more low alcohol than low calorie, and the thought was that if Hans or Fritz was the designated driver he could still keep up with his drinking buddies while only ingesting about half of the alcohol. Originally the German lights mimicked their American counterparts in that they were variations of Pilsner or helles. It wasn't long before some marketing genius came up with the idea of brewing light weissbier, or light Kölsch.

The light variations of Kölsch, as well as all of the German light, or *leicht,* beers, have fallen into the 7 to 8 °Plato starting gravity range. German beers are still typically

---

*The FDA actually regulates the labeling, and thus the production, of American light beers by saying that they must have at least 25% fewer calories than their "mother" brands. The alcohol content of these beers must also be in the range of 2.3 to 3.2% by weight.

brewed in one of the four starting gravity classes outlined in the beer tax law. There is a 3 °Plato gap between *schankbier* and vollbier on the upper end, and a 2 °Plato gap between schankbier and *einfachbier* on the lower end. The alcohol content of the German light beers is usually in the range of 2.5 to 3.5% by volume. The terminal gravity of these beers is in the range of 1.3 to 3 °Plato. In many cases brewers will add specialty malts such as CaraPils to the grist of a light beer to compensate for the lack of body, resulting from a lower starting gravity.

Alcohol-free beers have followed roughly the same path that light beers have in Germany, including the introduction of alcohol-free Kölsch. The starting gravity of these beers falls in either the einfachbier or schankbier gravity categories. By law, a nonalcoholic beer in Germany cannot have more than 0.5% alcohol by weight.

Color

There is nothing that compares to the gold color produced from an all-malt beer made with pale or Pilsner malt. Kölsch is no exception, and if ever the term *straw-gold* applied to the color of a beer, it would perfectly describe the color of Kölsch. Bavarian helles beer is a deeper gold than a Kölsch or a German Pilsner. This is mainly due to a slightly higher starting gravity and the fact that many helles brewers will decoct their mashes, thus deepening the color of the beer. Many Kölsch brewers, however, also decoct their mashes, so the darker Kölsch beers are likely to be decoction mashed. The color of a Kölsch is typically in the 7 to 14 EBC range (3.5 to 7 SRM). Advances in brew-house technology and techniques over the past 30 years have helped German brewers in their quest to brew pale beers without using adjuncts. Low oxygen pickup during mashing, lautering, and wort handling, as well as reduced wort boiling times, have played a major role in keeping the color of pale German beers as close to straw-gold as possible.

Bitterness

The 8 to 9 °Plato Kölsch of yesteryear was most noted as an extremely hoppy beer. A book published in 1938 describes this beer not as Kölsch, but as hop-bitter lager beer (the lager refers simply to the fact that this top-fermented beer was cold aged, not that it was brewed with a lager yeast) (Schönfeld 1938, 164). This style of top-fermented beer was prevalent not only in Cologne, but throughout the Rheinland. This beer was compared to the pale ales of England, but it was generally considered to be of a lower starting gravity than the English beers. More than a pound of hops per barrel was added to the nineteenth-century variety of Kölsch. Even though this was before the advent of high alpha-acid hops, this is a mouth-puckering, throat-constricting amount of hops, particularly if the starting gravity of these beers was in the 8 to 9 °Plato range. A pound-per-barrel hop addition for a barley wine may be just right, but for a low gravity beer like the hop-bitter lager beer, it would probably be out of balance. As if the high level of boil hops wasn't enough to give this beer its decidedly hoppy character, many of these beers were also dry hopped!

Today's Kölsch is a much more balanced beer that still has a distinctive hop character. All Kölsch beers are made with German variety bittering and aroma hops, such as Hallertau, Tettnang, Perle, and Hersbrucker. The bitter units (BU) for Kölsch today range from 16 on the low end to as high as 34. The BU for most Kölsch beers tend to be concentrated in the mid-20s. Most examples of Kölsch have a perceptible, but by no means dominating, hop aroma.

pH/Acidity

The normal pH of a Kölsch can range from 4.2 to as high as 4.7. Indeed, top-fermented beers will generally have a lower pH than lager beers. Any acidity that is detected while enjoying a Kölsch should be very faint, otherwise the beer is probably infected. The pH of the light and alcohol-free Kölsch tends to be slightly higher than that of the full-strength versions.

Carbonation

Kölsch is definitely more lightly carbonated than American lagers, and is carbonated to the same levels that most German beers are. The difference in carbonation levels between bottled and draft Kölsch can be as high as 0.5 volumes (0.1% by weight). On the low end, Kölsch that is gravity dispensed from a wooden barrel will have a carbon dioxide content of 2.05 volumes (0.4% by weight). On the high side, a bottled Kölsch will have carbonation levels nearing 2.65 volumes (0.52% by weight). The bottled versions feel wonderful as they slide down the gullet, but draft Kölsch that is more lightly carbonated is exceptionally drinkable.

Draft Kölsch, whether it is gravity dispensed or pushed with carbon dioxide, needs to have a lower carbonation level because it is served much warmer than American beer typically is. Kölsch is generally dispensed at temperatures between 45 and 50 °F (8 to 10 °C), and it would be very difficult to dispense a beer with a carbon dioxide content as high as 2.6 to 2.7 volumes at temperatures that warm. Most Kölsch beers are naturally carbonated in aging tanks. The Biersteuergesetz requires that beers can only be artificially carbonated if the carbon dioxide is reused from the individual brewery's carbon dioxide recovery plant. Since many smaller breweries can't justify the cost of a carbon dioxide recovery plant, artificially carbonating a beer isn't even an issue.

Fermentation By-Products of Kölsch

In the world of top-fermented beers, Kölsch is relatively muted in the expression of the fermentation by-products that characterize the estery, flowery, fusel-like, and even phenolic or diacetyl-like aroma and flavor profiles of some of the world's great ales. The relatively low level of fermentation by-products in Kölsch beer is, to a certain extent, a function of the brewing process. Specifically, fermenting Kölsch on the cool end of top ale yeast fermentation temperatures keeps the development of esters and higher alcohols in check. Long, cold aging of Kölsch ensures that the presence of acetaldehyde or diacetyl is reduced and kept at minimum levels, in addition to contributing greatly to the soft, round character of a well-made Kölsch. What seems to have the greatest influence on the spectrum of fermentation by-products in Kölsch is the yeast that is used to brew it. Table 2 compares data from a four-yeast experiment—incorporating Kölsch, weizen, alt, and lager yeasts—to data on six Kölsch beers.

The data in table 2 is from *German Wheat Beer* (Warner 1992, 49–50) and from the analysis of the six beers we have looked at throughout this chapter. Unfortunately, the fermentation parameters of the six Kölsch beers are largely unknown, but the parameters used for the experiment with the four different yeasts attempted to isolate as much information as possible down to the yeast strain. The same worts were fermented isothermally (i.e., the same fermentation temperature for the duration of the fermentation) at 59 °F (15 °C) in open, experimental fermenters.

It is truly striking what a tremendous impact the yeast strain has on the fermentation by-products of different beers. It is worth noting that the fermentation temperature of 59 °F (15 °C) is eight to eleven degrees Fahrenheit (four to six degrees Celsius) higher than normal production conditions for the lager yeast and as much as thirteen degrees Fahrenheit (seven degrees Celsius) lower than production conditions for the top-fermented beers. In other words, the normal fermentation temperatures for

TABLE 2

Influence of Yeast Type on Development of Fermentation By-Products (all concentrations in mg/l)

Fermentation By-Product (Characteristic Flavor or Aroma)	Threshold Level in German Lagers
Propanol-1 (fusel/solventlike)	
2-methyl-propanol-1 (fusel/solventlike)	> 10
2-methyl-butanol-1 (fusel/solventlike)	20–70
3-methyl-butanol-1 (fusel/solventlike)	20–70
Sum of higher aliphatic alcohols (fusel/solventlike)	
2-phenyl ethanol (rose or rose oil)	> 30
Ethyl acetate (solventlike [acetone], flowery in lower concentrations)	25–30
Iso-amyl acetate (very fruity, banana)	1–1.6
Acetic acid 2-phenyl ethyl ester/phenyl ethyl acetate (rose or honey)	
Hexanoic acid ethyl ester/ethyl caproate (fruity, winy)	0.12–0.23
Octanoic acid ethyl ester/ethyl caprylate (fruity, winy)	> 0.2
Decanoic acid ethyl ester/ethyl caprate (fruity, winy)	
Sum of fatty acid esters	
Caproic acid (goaty, yeasty)	
Caprylic acid (goaty, yeasty)	10–13
Capric acid (goaty, yeasty)	10
Sum of fatty acids	
Diacetyl (butter, butterscotch, toffee)	0.10–0.15
Pentanedione	
Acetoin	

[a]The numbers in the third column of the table reflect averages of data derived from the experiment with six Kölsch beers.

Six Kölsch Beers[a]	FOUR-YEAST STUDY			
	Kölsch Yeast	Weizen Yeast	Alt Yeast	Lager Yeast
	12.6	18.3	13.7	13
	8.9	34.8	10.2	11.1
	10.5	14.7	12	16.8
	38.6	44.8	46.2	35.7
82.5	70.6	112.6	82.1	76.6
27	33.7	42.1	30.5	43.9
	17.9	20.2	18.5	13.8
	1.57	1.69	1.78	1.27
	1.21	1.5	1.16	1.69
	0.15	0.15	0.17	0.16
	0.18	0.16	0.24	0.2
	0.01	0.01	0.02	0.02
0.72				
	1.16	0.88	1.42	1.06
	3.96	2.72	4.59	3.13
	0.24	0.05	0.26	0.26
11.1				
0.05				
0.015				
1.93				

lagers are 48 to 52 °F (9 to 11 °C), and 64 to 72 °F (18 to 22 °C) for most ales. The data pertaining to higher alcohols for the beer made with the Kölsch yeast in the four-yeast experiment and the six Kölsch beers is somewhat contradictory. The sum of the higher aliphatic alcohols is 17% higher in the six Kölsch beers than it is for the beer made with the Kölsch yeast in the four-yeast experiment. Considering that the analysis data from the six beers represents normal production conditions, this difference is not tremendously surprising. There is a strong correlation between fermentation temperature and the level of higher alcohols that is developed. It is reasonable to assume that the six beers were fermented at temperatures higher than 59 °F (15 °C), which was the fermentation temperature for the Kölsch yeast in the four-yeast experiment, thus higher levels of esters and higher alcohols are expected.

What is surprising is that the average level of 2-phenyl ethanol is lower among the six production beers than it is for the Kölsch yeast beer fermented at 59 °F (15 °C). Two of the six beers did have concentrations of 2-phenyl ethanol that were higher than the 33.7 milligrams per liter (mg/l), which were found in the beer made with the Kölsch yeast, but generally the expectation is that the higher the fermentation temperature, the higher the concentration of 2-phenyl ethanol. Again, the fermentation temperatures of the six production beers are not known, but it is reasonable to assume that, on average, they were higher than 59 °F (15 °C). What is significant about the data for 2-phenyl ethanol is that the comparison of the six-beer data or the data from the four-yeast experiment clearly shows that Kölsch has low levels of higher alcohols for a top-fermented beer. These results are congruent with what the Kölsch drinker expects: it is not a very alcoholic beer. Higher alcohols are seldom perceived in the aroma or flavor of Kölsch beers. If they are, it is probably indicative of a brewing mishap, such as too high a fermentation temperature, wort amino-acid concentrations that are too high or too low, improper pitching rates, or improper wort aeration levels prior to pitching.

Kölsch is described as having a slight fruity-estery aroma profile. The terms *winy* or *vinous* have also been used to describe the aroma and flavor profile of Kölsch. The data from the four-yeast experiment in table 2 seems to support these common descriptions of the flavor and aroma profile of Kölsch. The ethyl-acetate concentrations of all four experimental beers are below the threshold level, but the iso-amyl acetate levels are right where one would expect them to be: at the low end of threshold for the lager, near the upper end for the Kölsch, and well above for the *weizen* and alt yeasts. The fatty acid esters, which are associated with a fruity/winy aroma, are right at the threshold levels for the Kölsch yeast in the four-yeast experiment, but above threshold in sum for the average of the data from the six production beers in table 2. This definitely supports the commonly used description of Kölsch having a winy or vinous character, in addition to the fruity character that is ascribed to most top-fermented beers.

Kölsch is about as "clean" an ale as there is. This could be why this style is so often erroneously referred to as a "hybrid" style. I have never been able to understand any scientific justification for something called a hybrid yeast. Yeasts are either top-fermenting or bottom-fermenting. They either have the ability to ferment raffinose or they don't. A hybrid *process* makes a bit more sense (i.e., fermenting on the cool side for a top-fermented yeast or the warm side for a lager yeast [steam beer]), but all non-wild-yeast beer fermentations are carried out with either *Saccharomyces cerevisiae* (top-fermenting yeast) or *Saccharomyces uvarum* (bottom-fermenting yeast). There is no gray (hybrid) area.

The relatively clean aroma profile of Kölsch is, as we have seen, largely yeast strain specific. Data from both the beer made from the Kölsch yeast in the four-yeast experiment and the six production Kölsch beers show that fatty acid levels are below threshold. Levels of diacetyl and pentanedione are also well below the threshold level. The development of 2-aceto-lactate, the precursor to diacetyl, is greater and more rapid in top-fermented beers than in lagers, but the reduction to diacetyl and acetoin is also more thorough as a result of the higher fermentation temperature and vigorous fermentations. A Kölsch with perceptible diacetyl is an infected Kölsch, or it was made with the wrong yeast strain. Acetaldehyde concentrations are also very low, a result of thorough and vigorous primary fermentations and lengthy periods of cold aging. Even though wheat is often used in the grist of a Kölsch beer, the phenolic characteristics that are critical to Bavarian weiss beers should not be perceptible in Kölsch. Although the flavor of Kölsch can be slightly acidic, it should in no way be a noticeably acetic or lactic type of sourness. All other off-flavors or aromas such as dimethyl sulfide (DMS), chlorophenols, extreme sulfuriness, or oxidation should not be perceptible in Kölsch.

CHAPTER 3

Brewing Kölsch

Ingredients

The ingredients necessary to brew a Kölsch that is true to style are relatively conventional and are readily available. The keys are:

- German Pilsner or German pale malt
- German hops
- Soft water or water with low residual alkalinity
- Top-fermenting yeast that is low in ester, diacetyl, and higher alcohol production, and that works well

at lower primary fermentation temperatures (i.e., 59 to 65 °F [15 to 18 °C])

Malts and Grain Bill

The grain bill for a Kölsch beer is about as simple as it gets. Some breweries will use 100% pale or Pilsner malt and others will add up to 20% malted wheat to the grist. The barley malt used to brew Kölsch should be made from two-row barley. Specialty malts are rarely used to make a Kölsch, but if I were going to use anything it would probably be CaraPils or CaraHell in proportions of 3 to 5% of the total grain bill. Pilsner malt is synonymous

with pale malt in Germany, and a typical Pilsner malt analysis is shown in table 3.

TABLE 3

Typical Analysis for German Pilsner Malt

Water content, %	4.5
Extract, as is, %	77.8
Extract, fine grind, % dry substance	81.3
Coarse-grind/fine-grind extract difference, %	1.5
Wort color, EBC (°Lovibond)	3.3 (1.7)
Protein, % by weight	10.9
Soluble protein, % by weight	0.7
Friability, %	87.4
Conversion time, minutes	10–15
pH of analysis wort	6.02

Important to the Kölsch brewer is a low malt color of around 3 EBC units and protein of 11% or less. The composition of the proteins is also important for the speed of fermentation and the spectrum of fermentation by-products produced. Kölsch brewers place great emphasis on the amount of amino acids that are in the wort prior to yeast pitching. Too few amino acids can lead to sluggish fermentation, increased diacetyl levels,

Milling.

and higher than desirable concentrations of higher alcohols. Too many amino acids in knockout wort can also lead to greater concentrations of higher alcohols.

In Germany the Biersteuergesetz allows the use of malted wheat, rye, or oats, as well as technically pure cane, beet, inverted, or starch sugar for the production of top-fermented beers. However, in the southern German states of Bavaria and Baden-Wuerttemberg, state law takes precedence and the use of sugars or coloring agents made from sugar is verboten. Oddly enough, sweeteners such as saccharin and dulcin are allowed, but beers made from these sweeteners may only have a starting gravity of less than 4 °Plato (*einfach* beer). Artificial sweeteners were allowed in 1916 during World War I as a result of raw material shortages—basically an effort to save on sugar. In 1927 this aspect of the beer tax law was more permanently integrated into Biersteuergesetz with the stipulation that the starting gravity of a beer could be no greater than 4 °Plato (Schönfeld 1938, 186).

In Cologne, the use of wheat in brewing has been practiced for centuries. In the past, brewers perhaps used wheat because it was the only grain available at certain times; however, today's Kölsch brewers use malted wheat to improve the body, mouthfeel, smoothness, and head retention of their beers. If Kölsch brewers choose to use wheat in their grist, it is usually in proportions of less than 20% of the total grain bill. (See table 4.)

TABLE 4

Typical Analysis for German Wheat Malt

Water content, %	5.5
Extract, as is, %	80.3
Extract, fine grind, % dry substance	85.2
Coarse-grind/fine-grind extract difference, %	1.8
Wort color, EBC (°Lovibond)	3.5 (1.8)
Protein, % by weight	11.8
Soluble protein, % by weight	0.8
Viscosity, CP	1.85
Conversion time, minutes	10–15
pH of analysis wort	6.1

The key items to look at for wheat malt are the protein content and the number of discolored kernels found in the malt. The protein content should be less than 13%, and the total number of red or purple kernels should be less than 3 per 100 grams of malt sample. Discolored kernels are indicative of fungus growth (usually fusarium mycotoxin), which has been strongly correlated to gushing, or the extreme fountaining of beer, when a bottle is opened. Wheat malt generally yields more extract per unit of weight measure than barley malt, thus it is important for a Kölsch brewer to carefully calculate the expected yield from the barley and wheat malts if both are used.

German malts are becoming more readily available for both the homebrewer and the commercial brewer in the United States and Canada. North American pale malt is a suitable substitute for German Pilsner malt, and pale malts from other European countries, such as Belgium, France, and England, will also work well to brew a Kölsch. If a non-German pale malt is used, the most important things to look out for are low color (< 4 EBC or 2 °Lovibond), low protein (< 11%), and that the malt was made from two-row barley.

Hops

Hop selection is important to brewing a true-to-style Kölsch. It is critical to use German hops to emulate the flavor and aroma profile of a Kölsch. By German hops I mean

German hops grown in Germany. There are many who would beg to differ with me on this, but American-grown German hops are not the same, and therefore will not produce the same aromas and flavors as German hops grown in Germany. Genetically they are the same, but the soils and growing conditions in the Pacific Northwest are different from those in Germany, particularly in the Yakima Valley. There are only four types of German hops to remember to successfully brew a batch of Kölsch: Hallertau and Perle for bittering, and Tettnang and Hersbrucker for aroma. Northern Brewer hops can be used as bittering hops, and Spalt hops will also work well as the aroma hops for a Kölsch brew. It would be interesting to try brewing a

Nürnberg hop market.

Kölsch using Saaz hops as the finishing hops. If you absolutely insist on using American hops to brew your Kölsch, then Mt. Hood makes a suitable boil hop, and American Tettnangs works for the finishing hops. Remember, don't add your aroma hops too late in the boil unless you really want a big hop aroma. It is advisable to add them 10 to 20 minutes before the end of the boil.

Kölsch Water

In many ways the brewers of Kölsch and the brewers of Pilsner attempt to create the same characteristics in their beers:

- Pale, straw-golden color
- Delicate, round mouthfeel and smooth drinkability
- Pure hop bitterness without any type of harsh, lingering bitterness
- Relatively low levels of fermentation by-products

All of these characteristics are greatly influenced by water quality, and much as the brewer of a German Pilsner treats his water to "soften" it or, more specifically, to reduce the residual alkalinity of the water, the Kölsch brewer uses water of low residual alkalinity to create the perfect Kölsch.

Low residual alkalinity is critical for brewers seeking to brew beers with a pale, golden color. The lower the alkalinity of the brewing water, the greater the acidity (i.e., the lower the pH) of the mash and wort. Lower mash and wort pHs translate to better protein coagulation and precipitation during the boil. They also yield a wort that is lower in tannins, and thus lighter in color. And, a lighter wort equals lighter beer. Kölsch brewers generally aim for a mash pH of 5.5 and a wort pH of 5.2 to minimize the effects of high mash pH as previously outlined.

The same phenomena have a significant impact on the mouthfeel and drinkability of a beer, as well as the quality of the bitterness. The more coagulable proteins that are left in a wort in the brew house, the greater the harsh, protein bitterness flavor in the beer. The same tannins that affect the color of beer also detrimentally influence its bitterness.

Higher wort pH translates to a slower fermentation with longer lag time. This problem is compounded by the same coagulable proteins and tannins that aren't removed during the boil and that block yeast cell walls and thus their ability to ferment the wort. Higher mash pH translates to reduced protein conversion and a lower level of free amino nitrogen in the wort. This can have an impact on the fermentation by-products of Kölsch, including increased concentrations of diacetyl and higher alcohols. Slow or sluggish fermentation can also lead to decreased yeast flocculation, which means beer filtration can be more difficult and expensive.

Due to the more vigorous fermentation pattern of top-fermenting yeast, the effects of high residual alkalinity have a greater impact on lagers than ales, but most Kölsch brewers still strive to keep the pH of their mash as low as possible (5.4 to 5.5). Most brewers who use the relatively hard water supply of Cologne will treat their water to lower the residual alkalinity of the water. Brewers in Cologne who use well water are fortunate enough to have a water source that is naturally low in residual alkalinity, obviating any need for water softening.

Those brewers not living in or near Cologne who want to brew Kölsch and have access to soft water supplies are fortunate enough to be able to use untreated water. (All public water supplies should be dechlorinated in some way, ideally by using activated charcoal systems, or by simply boiling the water for smaller scale brewing.) Brewers living in areas where the water is hard, or in particular, high in carbonate hardness, have to treat the water in some way to lower the residual alkalinity of the brewing water. The simplest way to do this is to compensate using gypsum ($CaSO_4$) or calcium chloride ($CaCl_2$). I recommend calcium chloride if the intention is to come up with a beer that is as soft and round as possible. Using gypsum tends to give beers an unusually dry character. Kölsch as a beer style tends to be on the dry side anyhow, so that is why I recommend using calcium chloride over gypsum to increase mash acidity. One nice benefit of using calcium sulfate is that the sulfate tends to accentuate hop aroma.

I can testify firsthand to the benefits of having a water source that is low in residual alkalinity and to its positive impact on brewing a Kölsch. At Tabernash Brewing Company we brewed a Kölsch using very soft surface water with low residual alkalinity from the Rocky Mountains. We used a Kölsch yeast obtained from Germany, and the results were marvelous. The beer had a pale golden color and a soft, round drinkability that made it quite a session beer.

Yeast

The most important of the ingredients needed to brew a Kölsch is the yeast, but then again, this really is true for most styles. Once again, lest there be any confusion, Kölsch is a top-fermented beer, and even though it is sometimes referred to as a hybrid style, the yeast used to ferment Kölsch is *Saccharomyces cerevisiae*. If you want to brew a Kölsch that is true to style, it's important to try to track down the right strain of top-fermenting yeast. A few known strains of *Saccharomyces cerevisiae* are used to ferment Kölsch. If you just want to try something different, a top-fermenting yeast that produces low concentrations of esters and higher alcohols will be fine.

If you really want to hit the bull's eye and brew an awesome Kölsch, I suggest obtaining the 177 strain from Germany. This is the most widely used Kölsch yeast in Germany. Other Kölsch brewers have their own proprietary strains that they have been culturing for years. The best source that I know of to obtain this yeast is the yeast bank at Weihenstephan (telephone: 011 49 8161 713470; fax: 011 8161 714181). I have experience using this yeast and can attest to its performance in brewing a Kölsch that is true to style. It is a very dusty, nonflocculating yeast that ferments fairly vigorously and settles extremely slow. It ferments well at lower temperatures, such as 55 to 59 °F (13 to 15 °C), and will not produce high levels of undesirable fermentation by-products at temperatures as high as 72 °F (22 °C).

As would be expected, bottom harvesting of this yeast does not yield much, unless adequate time is allowed for the yeast to sediment. At Tabernash Brewing Company, we actually top-cropped the 177 yeast successfully from open fermenters in copious quantities. We skimmed the yeast from the surface of the fermenting beer, using a skimmer with a perforated head that was approximately 16 inches in diameter. Top-cropping the yeast in this way was best done when the beer was about two-thirds attenuated, or when the gravity of the beer reached approximately 5 °Plato.

If obtaining a Kölsch yeast from Germany is a daunting or financially unfeasible task, try some of the domestic yeast suppliers. Most of them have a Kölsch or alt yeast to recommend.

Mashing Techniques for Kölsch

Earlier versions of Kölsch were almost always exclusively single-infusion mashed, including our hop-bitter lager beer. Today, many brewers use a single decoction mash to brew their Kölsch. Mash-in temperatures vary widely depending on malt quality and desired wort composition. If malt quality dictates that a more intensive step mash or decoction mash program is in order, then mash-in temperature can be as low as 111 °F (44 °C). If the malt is well modified and/or the brewer is looking to make a soft, delicate Kölsch that is very pale and smooth, then he or she will use a step mash program with a mash-in temperature of 146 °F (63 °C). Generally, brewers of Kölsch strive for a level of alpha amino nitrogen in the hopped wort that corresponds to pale lager worts, in other words, 21 to 23 mg/l of 12 °Plato wort.

Given the high modification of most German pale malts today, it is surprising that some Kölsch brewers still decoction mash. The quality of Pilsner malts is good enough today that a decoction mash is overkill. I think decoction mashes are in order for darker, maltier beers and for certain types of wheat beer, where the intensive decoction mashing scheme helps to break down the complex proteins in the wheat. I can't imagine using a decoction mash to brew a Kölsch, considering the high level of modification among pale malts today. This is especially true with North American malts, which tend to be very well modified. They are also high enough in protein content that achieving high enough levels of free amino nitrogen in the wort isn't a great challenge. At Tabernash Brewing we used a step mash program to produce a great Kölsch. Using a decoction mash program for that beer probably would have only made it darker and grainier.

In fact, in the interest of thick beer foam, the decoction mash may be detrimental. Most Pilsner brewers bypass the protein conversion temperatures (116 to 126 °F/47 to 52 °C) altogether to leave as much of the high and middle molecular weight proteins intact as possible.

These middle and high molecular weight proteins are the essential building blocks for a dense, rocky head of foam. Also, transferring the mash one more time results in additional oxygen pickup. Oxygen uptake during the mash and lauter process has been correlated with longer lauter times, increased beer color, and a broad, tannic type of bitterness in packaged beer—product characteristics the Kölsch brewer tries to avoid. Despite modern brew-house technology that minimizes oxygen pickup during wort production, the fact remains that transferring the mash more than necessary usually translates into mash/wort oxidation.

In contrast to single-temperature infusion mashes, Kölsch step mashes often go through a variety of temperature ranges before going to the lauter tun. This touches on a fundamental difference between the Kölsch brewer and many of the British or American ale brewers. The brew house in Cologne usually has a dedicated mash kettle from which the mash is transferred to a dedicated lauter tun just prior to runoff. This is a practical necessity for brewers wanting to subject their mash to a multitemperature infusion or decoction mash program.

Mash Programs for Kölsch

Mash procedures for Kölsch aren't particularly difficult, but keeping a few ground rules in mind will definitely benefit the sensory profile. Remember, some of the key characteristics of a Kölsch that are influenced by mash procedure are: its pale, golden color; its soft, round flavor; and a dry character that is primarily a result of a high degree of attenuation.

First of all, it is important to mash with as little mash oxidation as possible. Mash oxidation can darken the color of the wort and give the beer a grainy and astringent character. This is accomplished by minimally splashing or agitating the mash. Second, I don't recommend using a decoction mash to brew your Kölsch. Decoction mashing will darken the color of a beer and it will probably produce a Kölsch that is somewhat maltier and grainier than an infusion-mashed Kölsch. Any of the readily available malts used to brew a Kölsch will be well modified to obtain good yields and desired conversion. Single-infusion mashing should work fine for your Kölsch, but I would recommend a step-infusion mash to be able to hit the beta- and alpha-amylase temperature optima of 143 to 149 °F (62 to 65 °C) and 156 to 167 °F (69 to 75 °C), respectively. Lautering should also be done with as little mash and wort splashing as possible, but this really holds true for brewing any beer, not just Kölsch.

Finally, it is best to try and brew a Kölsch with as thin a mash as possible. The greater volume of first runnings that can be collected, the less sparge water will have to be used. This should yield a beer that is more delicate and less grainy, because the husks aren't being washed out as much as they would be with a thicker mash. Many undesirable tannins are in the barley husks, and the more they are leached out by excessive sparging, the greater the concentration of tannic substances in the wort. Many Kölsch brewers will use a liquor to grist ratio of 4:1 by weight for mash-in. Mash/lauter tuns with wedge-wire screens usually don't perform well with mashes that thin, but it is still in the best interest of the beer to try and minimize the amount of sparging that occurs. Generally, Kölsch brewers stop sparging when the pH of the last runnings climbs over 6, or the gravity of the runnings drops below 2 °Plato. Sparge water should be between 170 and 175 °F (77 and 79 °C).

A multitemperature infusion mash program that goes through protein and starch conversion temperatures might be mashed in at 111 °F (44 °C) and then heated to 122 °F (50 °C) for a 20-minute protein rest. Next, this mash is heated to 143 °F (62 °C) and rested for 30 minutes. Kölsch brewers want to create as much fermentable extract as they can to drive the apparent degree of attenuation to more than 80%. A long maltose rest is critical to this end; that is, the mash should be rested at temperatures between 143 to 149 °F (62 to 65 °C) for 20 to 30 minutes. Next this mash might be heated to 159 °F (71 °C) for a 10- to 15-minute saccharification rest. After the brewer conducts an iodine test to make sure conversion is complete, the mash is heated to 170 to 173 °F (77 to 78 °C) for the mash-off temperature.

A simpler, less-intensive variation on this theme is to mash-in at 143 °F (62 °C) and continue the mash as just described. This is definitely recommended if the malt is well modified and has a high level of soluble protein. A protein rest is unnecessary if the soluble protein level is more than 600 to 650 mg per 100 grams (g) dry substance. This mash program yields a beer with outstanding foam characteristics.

I am not aware of any Kölsch brewery in Germany that doesn't employ at least a step mash program. But since so many North American breweries do not have systems that allow them to mash any other way than single infusion, it is important to discuss how to best brew a Kölsch following that mash procedure. Basically, the name of the game is to develop as much fermentable extract as possible, therefore a mash-in temperature of 143 to 149 °F (62 to 65 °C) is the target. As I have already mentioned, in most cases it will be difficult to execute this single-infusion mash with a lot of mash-in liquor. After holding the mash at the conversion temperature for 30 to 60 minutes, sparging begins with water that is between 170 and 175 °F (77 and 79 °C).

We've already determined that decoction mashing is probably overkill for a Kölsch, but since many Kölsch brewers still employ the decoction mash, it is important to review the basics of single decoction mashing. Typically the mash-in temperature is 98 to 113 °F (37 to 45 °C). Although no proteolytic or amylolytic enzyme activity occurs at these low mash-in temperatures, the purpose of the low mash-in temperature is to bring all of the enzymes into solution before the mash is heated to the temperatures where protein or starch conversion occurs.

After mash-in, one of two variations of the single decoction mash happens. More commonly, the Kölsch brewer heats the mash to the range of proteolytic enzyme activity (116 to 126 °F/47 to 52 °C), holds for 10 to 20 minutes, and then heats the mash to the temperature level where beta-amylase activity occurs. The temperature rise is usually at a rate of about one degree Celsius per minute. Once at the beta-amylase temperature range (143 to 149 °F/62 to 65 °C), a rest of 10 to 20 minutes is held before the decoction mash is pulled. Usually the thickest 40% of the mash is pulled for the decoction mash. The theory is that by pulling the thickest part of the mash: (1) a greater proportion of enzymes is left behind in the "soupier" part of the mash, and (2) it is the thick mash where the greater proportion of malt matter is that will be physically broken down for further starch conversion once the mashes are recombined. This thick mash is brought to a boil at a rise rate of one degree Celsius per minute and then boiled for 10 to 20 minutes. At the end of the boil, the mashes are recombined and the temperature of the whole is thus raised to saccharification temperatures (156 to 167 °F/69 to 75 °C). After a saccharification rest of 10 to 15 minutes, the mash is heated to the mash-off temperature of 169 to 171 °F (76 to 77 °C).

A less common variation of the single decoction mash emphasizes the protein rest, but is essentially the same, basic mash program as just outlined. The mash-in temperatures are similar, but instead of resting for a shorter period of time at the protein rest temperature range, the decoction mash is actually pulled while the main mash is at 116 to 126 °F (47 to 52 °C). Before the decoction mash is actually pulled, a short rest of 10 to 15 minutes may be employed. Again, 40% of the thickest part of the mash is pulled, heated to the beta-amylase temperature range, and held for 10 to 15 minutes. Afterwards, the mash is heated to 156 to 167 °F (69 to 75 °C) for a saccharification rest of 10 to 15 minutes before it is brought to a boil. After boiling the mash for 10 to 15 minutes, it is recombined with the main mash to raise the temperature of the whole to 143 to 149 °F (62 to 65 °C). After holding the mash at this temperature for 10 to 15 minutes, the mash temperature is raised to saccharification temperatures until conversion is complete, and then it is raised to mash-off temperature.

There is nothing extraordinary about lautering a Kölsch wort. The two points that are worth reiteration are: (1) the thinner the mash the better—as less sparging will be required, and thus the concentration of tannins in the wort will be lower; and (2) sparging should cease once the pH of the last runnings rises above 6 and/or the gravity of the last runnings dips below 2 °Plato, whereby the pH criterion is more important to observe.

Wort Boiling and Hopping

Wort boiling times are fairly normal, ranging from 60 to 100 minutes. A vigorous boil is essential to precipitate coagulable proteins and tannins. If you're brewing at lower elevations, 70 minutes should be plenty; if you happen to be lucky enough to be brewing at an elevation greater than 6,000 feet, you'll probably want your boil to be closer to 100 minutes to minimize the development of DMS.

Wort boiling.

As mentioned earlier, hop additions have been dramatically reduced compared to the hop-bitter lager beer. Anywhere from 7 to 14 g of alpha acid per hectoliter (hl) of wort are added to the kettle. If the average alpha-acid content of the hops used is around 6%, this translates to roughly one-quarter to one-half pound per barrel. Generally you will probably want to use about two-thirds of the total alpha acids of the hops (or two-thirds of the total bittering power of the hops) for the boil and one-third for the aroma dosage. The first addition of hops is typically at the beginning of the boil or 15 minutes into it. Hallertau and Perle hops are commonly used as bittering hops, and often the addition of the bittering hops is in the form of hop extract (not isomerized extracts, as they are illegal under the Biersteuergesetz). The hop extracts are often more stable, consistent products that require less storage space than leaf or pellet hops. Aroma hops are customarily added 10 to 20 minutes before the end of the boil. Frequently used aroma hops include Tettnang and Hersbrucker, although Perle and Spalt are also sometimes employed as finishing hops. Pellets or cones will work fine. I recommend pellets because Kölsch isn't a "hoppy" style. There is no need for using fresh cones and a hop back or anything like that. Do make sure that your hops are fresh, as any rancid or cheesy aroma is not true to style.

Hot trub from a Kölsch brew is removed using a whirlpool or centrifuge. I recommend a 15- to 20-minute whirlpool rest before beginning the runoff of the wort. To keep levels of DMS as low as possible in finished beer, it is important to cool the wort in 90 minutes or less. Many breweries also attempt to remove some level of cold trub. Cold trub separation tends to give a beer a "cleaner" bitterness that is derived mainly from hop bitterness, not protein bitterness. Cold trub separation is almost always used for lager beer production, and since

Wort cooling.

Kölsch is a top-fermented lager, so to speak, many brewers choose to separate the cold trub from the wort. The common methods used to remove cold trub are wort filtration, cold sedimentation, flotation, or a starting tank. As one might infer, cold trub separation occurs after the wort has been chilled. For small brewery applications, cold sedimentation is probably the simplest method of separating cold trub. The key to cold sedimentation is to find the sweet spot between letting the trub have enough time to settle while still separating the beer from the sedimented trub and dead yeast cells before fermentation becomes active. I have used flotation before for lager and

Kölsch production. Basically, the wort is saturated with sterile air (not oxygen, as the amount of oxygen necessary to create the degree of foaming for successful flotation has a toxic effect on the yeast) to the point where a thick layer of foam forms on the surface of the wort in the flotation tank. As air bubbles rise, cold trub particles are carried to the surface of the wort, and after two to five hours the wort is then drained from the tank into a fermenter, leaving the cold trub behind. The yeast can be pitched during or after flotation.

CHAPTER 4

Fermentation, Maturation, and Packaging

Yeast Pitching

Pitching rates vary for Kölsch between 0.25 to 1.5 l/hl of wort. This corresponds to approximately 6 to 40 million cells per milliliter (cells/ml) (Narziss 1986, 353). This range is very wide and it represents the extremes of what breweries may have traditionally used, but today most breweries will strive to pitch in the range of 10 to 20 million cells/ml. Modern yeast management techniques have gone a long way toward narrowing the range to the 10 to 20 million cells/ml.

Without digressing into an extensive discussion, there are a few key points to observe regarding yeast management. Repitching as soon as possible after cropping is very important. This keeps the yeast in an active state metabolically and is less likely to lead to sluggish fermentations and development of undesirable fermentation by-products, such as diacetyl or fusel alcohols. If the yeast can't be repitched within one to two days, it is a good idea to store the yeast cold (34 to 37 °F/1 to 2 °C) in water. This method of yeast storage generally works well if repitching will occur within seven days. For longer periods, it is a good idea to feed the yeast every five to seven days with lower gravity wort (< 10 °Plato). This helps to keep the yeast active before it is repitched. In this case it is also good to aerate the wort as well. The wort fed to the yeast should constitute about 10 to 20% of the volume of yeast and it should be warm (68 °F/20 °C). If this is not possible, the wort used to feed the yeast should be well aerated. Some modern pitching techniques involve an intense aeration of the yeast, without actually aerating the wort! This is something that can only be done under very controlled conditions, however. Unless you are top-cropping your yeast and reusing it right away, I don't recommend employing the yeast beyond six to ten generations.

With the higher pitching rates, aeration is less, but otherwise Kölsch worts are normally aerated. The high end (> 20 million cells/ml) also probably indicates yeast that has low viability or has been acid washed. Typical rates of aeration prescribe 7 to 10 mg/l of oxygen. Pitching temperatures are usually in the 53 to 72 °F (12 to 22 °C) range (Narziss 1986, 353).

Fermentation and Aging

The classic Kölsch fermentation took place in an open fermenter, often at temperatures as low as 48 to 56 °F (9 to 13 °C). These fermentations were reputed to have taken six to seven days with high degrees of attenuation. The brewers 100 years ago knew that bringing the temperature of the primary fermentation down to these low temperatures brought the beers closer to a lager type of character. At temperatures this low the fermentation activity must have been akin to the pulse of a bear in hibernation. In this sense, it is perhaps fair to label the Kölsch yeast as a hybrid yeast. Maybe after years and years and hundreds or thousands of generations, the Kölsch yeast started working well at lower temperatures, or perhaps the yeast had always been suited to the lower fermentation temperatures.

These cooler temperatures gave the beer a roundness and a long-lasting dense head. The brews weren't cooled down too far, as the brewers recognized that this would totally inhibit any fermentation activity of the yeast in the aging cellars. Prior to the widespread use of refrigeration technology, brewers of hop-bitter lager beer tried as hard as possible to age the beer at 37 to 45 °F (3 to 5 °C) to get as much carbon dioxide into solution, eliminate as many colloidal substances, and give the beer the greatest protection against bacterial development as possible. These beers were lagered two to three months, usually at temperatures between 41 and 45 °F (5 and 7 °C) (Schönfeld 1938, 165–66). Before the advent of modern refrigeration, aging beer was kept cool by using subterranean aging cellars that were kept cold with ice. The ice was "harvested" in the winter and maintained in underground ice storage rooms. Fermentations were not controlled, and this is why the traditional brewing calendar was from late September through April. It would simply be too hot in the summer for fermentations to be kept at temperatures low enough to keep the beer from spoiling or developing undesirable fermentation by-products.

The wooden, open fermentation vessels of old have by and large made way for huge, multiple-brew, cylindro-conical tanks that can be as high as a six-story building. Expensive real estate and inventory costs have accelerated the Kölsch brewing process somewhat, but many breweries still ferment cold and age long. Today, many Kölsch brewers ferment in the 64 to 68 °F (18 to 20 °C) range. The larger breweries will brew multiple batches in a single fermenter, sometimes as many as 12 over the course of 24 hours. Often these huge fermentation tanks are capped and vented at 0.6 to 0.7 bar (8 to 10 psi). So-called pressure fermentation helps to counteract the effects that higher fermentation temperatures tend to have on beer, such as higher levels of esters and higher alcohols. It also serves to begin the saturation of carbon dioxide in the beer at an early juncture in the fermentation. The trick to executing a successful pressure fermentation is to raise the pressure of the tank as the amount of fermentable extract in the fermenter decreases. If the pressure is raised too early, yeast reproduction is throttled and the fermentation will proceed too slowly. If the pressure build-up occurs too late or is not high enough, the level of fermentation by-products will be too high (Narziss 1986, 260). After budding has occurred, the pressure in the tank is raised to about 0.3 bar (4.2 psi). Once the beer is approximately 50% attenuated, the pressure is raised to as high as 1.8 bar (25 psi). Pressure fermentations require tight management, and I don't recommend doing it unless you have experience

Transferring beer between vats with handpump.

with it. A major reason not to use a pressure fermentation is the complexity of yeast cropping. The yeast has to be cropped under pressure, otherwise it will be severely damaged going from 1.8 bar (25 psi) to atmospheric pressure. Usually, the yeast will be harvested into a pressure tank, and then the pressure will be slowly reduced to minimize the yeast damage.

Another way of keeping fermentation by-products, such as diacetyl and esters, at lower levels is to pump multiple brews into one fermenter, or double. Doubling also ensures a rapid primary fermentation, and after three days the primary fermentation is complete. The trick to doubling is to make sure that the yeast has not entered into anaerobic metabolism. This can be regulated by varying the pitching rate, the level of aeration of the initial brews, as well as the brews that are being doubled into the tanks, and the temperature of the fermentation during the lag phase. Again, I don't recommend doubling without having had some prior experience with the practice.

On the fourth day of fermentation, assuming the beer is at or near end attenuation, the beers are sometimes subjected to a one-day diacetyl rest, and on the fifth day the brew is cooled to 37 to 40 °F (3 to 4 °C). Diacetyl rests are more commonly used with lager yeasts or with top-fermenting yeasts that tend to produce diacetyl. A typical diacetyl rest customarily involves raising the temperature of the beer to 64 to 72 °F (18 to 22 °C), but because a Kölsch is usually fermented at this temperature anyhow, the diacetyl rest is as simple as leaving the beer at the fermentation temperature for an extra day after it is end-attenuated.

Once the beer is end-attenuated, with or without a diacetyl rest, it is ready to be cooled. Many Kölsch breweries cool the beer to cold-aging temperatures (30 to 34 °F/ -1 to 1 °C) within 24 hours. I believe it is better to step the beer down to this temperature slowly over a period of three to four days. My experience has been that this produces a smoother, more mature beer. At this point, the beer may be transferred to an aging tank, or a uni-tank process may be carried out and the beer will stay put. In either case the beer is aged at 32 to 30 °F (0 to -1 °C) to settle out as much yeast and eliminate as many colloidal proteins as possible. If the beer is transferred to an aging tank, it is often centrifuged en route to reduce the cell count to three to eight million cells/ml of beer. This ensures that there is enough yeast in the beer for the maturation cycle, but not so much that the beer develops a yeasty character. Green-beer centrifugation is all the more important the higher the yeast count, the longer the aging time, and the warmer the aging temperature. If you transfer your beer from a primary fermenter into an aging vessel, it may be necessary to let your Kölsch settle out for a period of one to four days after primary fermentation to ensure that there is not too much yeast going with the beer into the aging tank. This is particularly true with the Kölsch yeasts because they tend to be nonflocculating anyway.

Many smaller Kölsch breweries still ferment and age their brews in a more traditional fashion. These breweries may still double into open fermenters, but usually only one to two times, mainly because open fermenters aren't practical at larger sizes (> 250 bbl). They will ferment on the cooler end at 57 to 65 °F (14 to 18 °C) for three to four days, cool to 46 to 50 °F (8 to 10 °C), and then transfer to an aging tank with 12 to 17% fermentable extract remaining in the green beer. Sometimes the green beer is transferred to the aging cellar without having been cooled from the primary fermentation temperature. The yeast from these brews is often top-cropped, but it is also bottom harvested after the beer has been transferred for aging. I believe the healthiest yeast is obtained from top-cropping. Top-cropped yeast always contains the healthiest cells of pure yeast. Bottom-cropped yeast generally contains more dead cells and hop resins.

The cell count of the green beer frequently ranges from 15 to 40 million cells/ml. The higher number may indicate a beer that will be transferred again from a warmer

Bunging a wooden aging tank.

aging cellar into a colder one after one to two weeks. Cold aging typically lasts one to two weeks, but some breweries still age their Kölsch as long as six to eight weeks. An aging scenario in this case entails a warm phase at 39 to 41 °F (4 to 5 °C) followed by a cold aging of 14 to 40 days at 32 to 30 °F (0 to -1 °C). During the aging process the tanks are bunged so that the beer is carbonated at the time of packaging. Of course, the bunging process is difficult if there is not enough fermentable extract in beer to produce carbonation. So, if you are going to attempt this, you can forget much of what you just read in the last few paragraphs. If you want to attempt bunging using a primary fermenter and an aging vessel, you will have to leave 1 to 2 °Plato of fermentable extract in the beer. This is difficult to do with top-fermented beers, so the most practical way to naturally carbonate your Kölsch is to: (1) use priming sugar or wort, or (2) allow pressure to build in the fermenter at the end of fermentation and then transfer the beer under pressure to the aging tank. Homebrewers will probably want to use priming sugar, and North American commercial brewers will most often force carbonate beer in the bright beer tank. In some cases the so-called falling bunging practice is employed. In that case the beer is bunged to a pressure of 0.8 to 1.2 bar

(11 to 17 psi) and then the pressure is slowly released until the set pressure is reached.

Clarification

Adequate aging times and temperatures help to settle out much of the yeast prior to packaging, but the highly nonflocculating character of Kölsch yeast means that Kölsch is a bit more difficult to filter than, for example, a lager. Prior to the widespread use of modern clarification equipment, such as filters and centrifuges, Kölsch beer was clarified with finings or wood chips. Today, the Biersteuergesetz allows finings for top-fermented beers, provided that they have a mechanical, not chemical, clarifying effect, and that they are fully separated from the beer prior to packaging.

Modern Kölsch brewers use diatomaceous earth and sheet filters to clarify their beers. Bottled beer is frequently filtered to the point of sterility (< 0.45 microns). Sometimes the beer will first pass through a centrifuge en route to the filtration equipment to allow for longer filtrations, thus minimizing diatomaceous earth usage and maximizing the labor expended on filtration. In some cases stabilizing agents, such as silica gels, are also used. Larger breweries distributing in an expanded radius require a bottled product with an extended shelf life, and stabilizing agents help dramatically to increase the chemical/physical stability of a beer. Homebrewers can use finings and/or gelatin to attempt to clarify their Kölsch.

The once popular wiess beer has undergone a resurgence in popularity in recent years. This is an unfiltered version of Kölsch, but it is not to be confused with Bavarian- or Berlin-style weiss beer. Many of the new generation's brewpubs in Germany have carved out a niche, serving unfiltered variations of popular styles, such as Pilsner, helles, and Kölsch.

Bottling at the turn of the century.

Packaging Kölsch

Kölsch comes packaged in just about any type of container you can imagine, from 33-centiliter bottles all the way up to the so-called Beer Drive tanks, which are basically large (10 to 50 hl), on-site serving tanks that are used for outdoor events attracting large crowds. Kölsch is even available in cans. Interestingly enough, there is an ongoing debate in Germany, and particularly in Bavaria, regarding the increasing use of cans as a beer package. The small- and medium-sized brewers claim the can is an environmental threat, because breweries in Germany typically rewash their bottles, collected through an extensive deposit system. The large breweries feel it is their duty to provide their customers with a convenient package, and because cans are lighter than bottles, shipping

costs are less for canned beer. Cans also offer more protection from light. The debate has escalated to the point that there has even been a suggestion of legislation regulating the use of cans in breweries; however, canning beer is kosher with the Biersteuergesetz. Whereas the majority of all beer sold in America is in cans, it is the opposite in Germany. So despite the increased presence of cans on the store shelf in Germany, you are still more likely to find your Kölsch in a bottle. That is, unless you are enjoying a draft Kölsch.

CHAPTER 5

The Fun Part:
Drinking Kölsch
and
Enjoying Cologne

Fearing God makes one blessed
Drinking beer makes one happy
Therefore, fear God and drink beer
and you will stay blessed and happy

—Anonymous

The Stange of Kölsch

What separates the bona fide beer styles of the world from the impostors or wanna-bes is the glass. Insipid swill can be served in the most generic glassware, but this classic

Kölsch

Stange.

beer style has its own distinctive glass. Weizen beer has its vase-shaped glass with a narrow bottom, real ales have the queen's pint, and Kölsch has the two-centiliter Stange. In fact, according to the Kölsch Konvention, "the producers of Kölsch will to the best of their abilities see that Kölsch will only be poured in the so-called 'Kölsch Stange' (Kölner Stange)." The prevailing theory is that the unique size and shape of the Stange prevents the beer from becoming too warm or going flat too soon after it is poured. The Stange holds a net volume of approximately seven ounces and is made of very thin glass. Net volume is to be differentiated from gross volume, because in Germany all glassware has a calibration mark below the rim of the glass, designed to protect the interests of the consumer. A beer in Germany should be poured to the level of the calibration mark and above it a rich head of meniscoid foam should tower over the rim of the glass.

For the waiter, or Köbes, in Cologne, the two-centiliter glass is a blessing and a curse. Smaller glassware translates to greater per ounce price that the customer pays. Assuming a customer will come into a pub and drink a certain amount of beer, regardless of the size of the pour, this translates to higher revenue. (Bavarian beer garden owners argue that it's better to sell an entire liter mug full of beer as opposed to five two-centiliter beers). On the other hand, the Köbesse in Cologne work harder to sell these higher priced beers, making two and one-half trips to the bar to serve the same amount of beer that a waiter or waitress in Bavaria could serve in one trip. The glass is also much thinner than even a Pils glass, let alone a sturdy Bavarian glass or mug, so increased breakage is common in pubs in Cologne. Also, more glasses have to be washed to serve the same amount of beer than in Bavaria. Nonetheless, the Stange is what Kölsch is served in, no matter which pub in Cologne you visit.

The Stange hasn't always been the glassware of choice in Cologne. The original beer mugs were called Pinten. (I've always said German is a really easy language to learn because of the sheer number of cognates it has to English).

Pinten.

105

Schnelle.

These were fired, clay mugs that did not always necessarily bear a resemblance to today's beer mugs or glasses. These Pinten were decorated simply and, more often than not, probably resembled a fifth grader's pottery project when it came to symmetry and sophistication of detail (Mathar/Spiegel 1989, 126–27). Hey, as long as it was beertight.

The next step in the evolution toward the Stange was the Schnelle. These tended to be tall, narrow mugs and were more reminiscent of today's concept of a beer mug. Also made of clay, the Schnelle was richly decorated, often with allegories. The Schnelle held more than a half liter of beer. As the Industrial Revolution gained momentum, so did the mass production of glassware. Before that time, beer drinkers drank from clay mugs, because glass was expensive and difficult to process. The birth of the glass Stange is generally accepted to have been at the end of World War I. After the war, there was a strong demand for glass, and the Kölner Stange was simple to mass produce quickly. Since that time, the drinking vessel of choice in Cologne has been the 0.2-liter, tall, cylindrical glass called the Stange. For special occasions Cologners will use hand-blown, etched Stangen.

Why Is My Waiter Wearing a Skirt?

Aside from the beer itself and the Stange, there is one common thread to any Kölsch pub: the Köbes. Yet another characteristic that reflects the depth of brewing tradition in Cologne, the Köbes is a lot more than just a waiter. To be a Köbes is somewhat of an honor, and you won't find the same type of turnover among the Köbesse as you will among other service staff. Originally the Köbes wore a blue knit waistcoat, a blue linen apron, and a leather money pouch covering the crotch area. The blue sweater has by and large given way to blue or white short-sleeved shirts, but the Köbes is still a fixture in all of the major brewpubs (in the expanded sense of the word) in Cologne.

The Köbesse were originally the brewery apprentices. In addition to their vocation in brewing, they also had to work in the tap rooms to learn how to get on with people "in the real world." The word *Köbes* is the Kölsch word for "Jakob" (Jacob). The story goes something like this: Many of the richer Cologners used to go to Santiago de Compostella in northern Spain on pilgrimages. This was called the path, or way, of Jacob, because they received a Jacob's shell as a reward for their efforts. The rich could afford the journey by carriage, but the apprentices could not. So, they would work in guest houses and pubs along the way doing the service work that they were known for. Colloquially, Köbesse became the phrase for "making money on the Jacob's pilgrimage."

The Köbesse can only be male. Naturally, this is not law, but in Europe the adherence to tradition sometimes still prevails over any notion of political correctness. The

Köbesse serve huge numbers of beers, in addition to any food they might bring to the table. Remember, in Cologne the common size for a draft beer is 200 ml. In Bavaria it is 500 ml, similar to a pint in the United States or United Kingdom. There is documentation of two Köbesse working at a pub around the turn of the century. Reportedly they served over 12,000 glasses of beer on busy Sundays. If we assume a 12-hour shift, that's

500 beers per Köbes, per hour, or almost 10 per minute. Things are a little less hectic today, but even the largest brewpubs have only a few Köbesse working the floor at any given time. They are not unfriendly per se, but there is no place for the indecisive or the teetotaling in a Kölsch pub. When the Köbes has a moment or two to spare, it is not uncommon that he will let his patrons buy him a quick beer. One of the reasons the Köbesse can be so efficient is that they only have one style of beer to serve. They don't have to worry about having 20 different beers on tap (Mathar/Spiegel 1989, 129–30).

How to Count 12,000 Beers in a Day

The coaster, aside from its immeasurable value as a marketing tool for breweries, has a very practical purpose for the Köbesse and servers all over Germany: marks are made around the outer edge of the coaster every time a round of beers is served. This is the way the Köbesse tabulate the number of beers consumed by a party or an individual. Even today, despite the advancements in point-of-sale computer systems for restaurants, most traditional pubs in Germany calculate the check total (at least for beers) in this way. When the guest is ready to pay, the Köbes will ask the guest to remind him what he or she ordered to eat and then count the number of marks on the coaster to calculate the amount to charge for the beers.

As is so often the case, today's customs have their roots in yesterday's practices. Before the advent of the paper coaster, the number of beers served was marked with chalk directly onto the table or onto the wall. When someone ordered a beer, he or she was "written up." If the customer paid, his or her name was erased, otherwise it "stood in the chalk." In the more "cultured" pubs, a beer was served with a porcelain saucer (see illustration on page 111). Each time the waiter cleared an empty glass, he would stack the saucer on top of the one he brought with the previous beer. When the guest was ready to leave, the waiter simply counted the number of saucers. Of course, there was also the obvious method of letting the empty glasses or mugs collect on the table. (Today over two billion beer coasters are produced worldwide every year.)

I Want to Have a Beer, Not Go to Church

One of the more truly unique elements to a true Kölsch pub is a confessional. As we've learned, there can be a strong connection between Christianity and brewing, but this confessional had another purpose. Literally more of an observation point, the *beichtstuhl* was typically

Der halven Hahn.

De mihste Freud der Kölsche hät,
Ov Bürgerschmann, ov Rhingkadett,
An echtem Wiess, we meer et han,
Un an 'em leck're »halven Hahn«.

Gruss aus Köln!

111

located between the hallway where the beer is poured and the main floor of the pub. It is normal to assume that a publican would observe the activity in his operation from behind the bar, but Kölsch pubs don't have bars. From the location of the beichtstuhl the publican could observe not only the pouring of the beer, but the activity on the main floor. In many cases the publican controlled the entire flow of food from the kitchen and beer from the taps from his "throne." There is still one Kölsch pub today where the publican inspects every order that goes out for quality and accuracy. Historians speculate that the concept of the beichtstuhl originated sometime in the last 200 years as traffic into the pubs increased dramatically. Although the beichtstuhl has by and large suffered the same fate as despotic management techniques, many pubs still have the original structure in place and some still use it for its intended purpose.

CHAPTER 6

Recipes for the Hobby Brewer and the Professional

In Germany, homebrewers are called hobby brewers, so I thought I would lend a little authenticity to this chapter title. One of the nice things about brewing a Kölsch is that the procedures and ingredients used are relatively simple. Kölsch brewers don't have to worry about complicated double mash or parti-gyle brewing techniques. Although fermentation temperature makes a difference in the flavor profile of a Kölsch, a 10-degree Fahrenheit or five-degree Celsius difference in brewing a Kölsch won't make nearly as much of a difference as it would in brewing a lager. In other words, take two identical batches of lager, but ferment one at 50 °F (10 °C) and the other at 59 °F (15 °C), and you will have quite a difference in terms of flavor and aroma profile. Take two identical batches of Kölsch and ferment one at 59 °F (15 °C) and the other at 68 °F (20 °C), and the difference in fermentation by-products won't be as appreciable.

At this point I'd like to review a few key points on brewing procedure to make sure your batch of Kölsch is the best it can be.

Fermentation

If you want your fermentation to go like clockwork, look for all the usual suspects: well-aerated wort; fresh, viable yeast that is biologically pure; proper pitching quantity; good trub separation; and a pitching temperature that is neither too low nor too high. I don't recommend using a pitching temperature that is much below 59 °F (15 °C). Depending on the consistency and viability of your yeast, I suggest pitching between a pint and a quart of yeast per barrel of wort. Relative to the inherent inclination of the yeast you've selected to produce certain fermentation by-products, the usual rules apply regarding your ability to control the level of fermentation by-products. If you want a Kölsch that is fruitier, ferment at higher temperatures (64 to 72 °F/18 to 22 °C), lower aeration levels, and try to ferment in shallow fermenters. If you want ester production to be low, ferment cooler (55 to 63 °F/13 to 17 °C); keep aeration levels normal; and ferment in closed, vertical fermentation tanks. Again, this is all relative to the yeast strain you use.

Carbonation and Packaging

In Germany it is fairly common to naturally carbonate Kölsch in the aging tanks. This is accomplished by leaving a certain amount of residual fermentable extract in the beer before the aging process begins. A good rule of thumb is to leave about 15% of the fermentable extract in the beer prior to aging. In very simple terms, if the starting gravity of the beer is 12 °Plato and the final gravity is 2 °Plato, you will want to start the aging/natural carbonation process when the beer is at about 3.5 °Plato. Homebrewers should definitely rack the beer off the lees into some type of aging vessel (another carboy or five-gallon keg). Commercial brewers can transfer to an aging tank, or if cylindro-conical fermenters are being used, aging can occur in the fermentation tank. In this case it is important to shoot off the yeast every week or so during conditioning. If you plan to carbonate your Kölsch in some way other than in the aging vessel, you may as well go ahead and end ferment the beer before aging, as the real purpose of leaving the residual extract in the beer is to carbonate it. Transferring the beer after the final gravity has been reached has the added benefit of bringing less yeast into the aging tank, which will minimize yeasty flavors in the finished product and, for those Kölsch brewers who choose to filter their beer, make filtration go more efficiently.

If you want to naturally carbonate your Kölsch, there are two ways to do it: in the tank or bottle condition. As we discussed in chapter 4, some Kölsch brewers will actually cap off the fermentation tank early in the fermentation to begin carbonation. I don't recommend this procedure unless you are applying a ton of science to your brewing. If the pressure in the fermenter gets too high, too soon, yeast reproduction will severely taper off and the fermentation will be slowed. Once the level of fermentable extract is below 20% of its original value, enough reproduction has occurred to safely begin building pressure in the tank. The bunging procedures for carbonating beer during aging were outlined in chapter 4. Bottle conditioning can occur using priming sugar, wort, or some other source of fermentable sugar. In my homebrewing exploits I have found that using wort as a primer gives my beers a better overall flavor and mouthfeel. With Kölsch you could look at it in two ways. Because it is a dry style, using priming sugar would be right in line, since it tends to have a drying effect on beers. On the other hand, because it is such a dry style, priming sugar could make the beer more watery and even drier. Your call.

Draft Kölsch should be carbonated at 2.2 to 2.4 volumes. If you want to try and do a "cask" Kölsch that will be hand pumped or gravity dispensed, carbonate to about 2 volumes, depending on the serving temperature (which is from 41 to 47 °F/5 to 8 °C). Bottled Kölsch is probably best carbonated to a level around 2.65 volumes, but that's up to you.

A Final Note

If your goal is to brew a Kölsch that is as true to style as possible, try to follow as many of these guidelines as possible. I have judged the Kölsch category at the Great American Beer Festival® (GABF℠) on more than one occasion, and the judges have often been hard pressed to find three medal-worthy beers. The results from this category over the last several years support my observation. In some years not all medals were awarded. Certainly, this is in part due to a small number of entries for the category. Let's face it, Kölsch is not exactly the most popular or well-known style among brewers and consumers in America. Nevertheless, the number of entries in the Kölsch category at the GABF has risen to a level where there should be three medal-worthy beers. My point is simply this: pale, delicately hopped beers are harder to brew than darker or more aggressively hopped beers. Bigger malt and hop flavors simply mask fermentation by-products and minor flavor nuances. It isn't usually any one minor deviation from a recipe that makes the final product different from what is desired, but the accumulation of many small deviations will make a noticeable difference. Good luck!

Recipe Formulation and Recipes

It is generally assumed that the lab yield for pale malted barley will be 78%, and for malted wheat 83% (air dry substance). A yield difference of +/- 5% is assumed between these theoretical values and what you can expect to get. These figures were chosen based on empirical observations; if they do not reflect the yield of your malt or the efficiency of your brewing process, adjust accordingly.

Hop additions are expressed in terms of grams of alpha acid to be added to the brew. It would be impractical, for example, to say "one-quarter pound of Perle," because of the variation in alpha acid content. This variation results from year to year differences in the hop harvest, as well as from the type of hop product used. Cone Perle may have any alpha-acid content of 5%, pellets 5.5%, and enriched pellets 10%. Arriving at the correct amount of hops to use is relatively simple math. Take the given grams of alpha acid per barrel or five gallons and divide by the percent alpha acid of the hop product you are using (use the decimal, not the whole percentage number; i.e., for 5% alpha acid, divide by 0.05). As an example, if the recipe calls for 4 g of alpha acid at the beginning of the boil using Perle, and the alpha-acid content of the Perle is 5%, divide 4 by 0.05, which equals 80 grams, or approximately 2.8 ounces of that hop. The homebrew bittering unit (HBU) takes this into account. To express in HBU for the same recipe, you multiply the 2.86 ounces by 5% to arrive at 14.3 HBU.

Lawnmower Kölsch (Extract)

This is a great, entry-level, extract recipe. It really doesn't get much easier than this, so use this recipe as an introduction to brewing Kölsch or as a chance to master your extract brewing skills.

Malt	5 Gallons	1 Barrel
Pale malt extract	7.5 lb. (3.4 kg)	46.5 lb. (21.1 kg)

Hops	5 Gallons	1 Barrel
Perle	1 g alpha acid	6.2 g alpha acid

Kölsch Specifications	5 Gallons	1 Barrel
Liquid Kölsch yeast:	4 oz. (120 ml)	24.8 oz. (720 ml)
Brewing water:	2 gal.	12.4 gal.

OG: 12 °P
BU: 27
ADF: 78%

Bring brewing water to boil, reduce heat, then dissolve the liquid or dry extract by stirring well. Once the extract is thoroughly dissolved, bring the brew pot to a boil. Once the pot is boiling again, add three-quarters of the Perle hops. Add the remaining one-quarter of the hops 45 minutes later. After the wort has boiled for one hour, turn off heat. Fill fermentation vessel with 3 gallons of cold water for a 5-gallon batch or 18.6 gallons of cold water for a 1-barrel batch and then add wort to fermenter. Try to keep as much trub as possible out of the fermenter, and splash the wort as it is going into the fermenter. Make sure the temperature of the wort is below 77 °F (25 °C) before adding the yeast. Try to ferment as close to 68 to 72 °F (20 to 22 °C) as possible. Ferment until the beer appears to be end-attenuated. Transfer to a secondary fermenter and allow to age for one week at cellar temperature or three weeks cold. Bottle using 3/4-cup priming sugar for 5 gallons. Store at room temperature for one week and then chill for two weeks before testing the results.

If you have a wort chiller, use 5 gallons of brewing water for a 5-gallon batch and 31 gallons for a 1-barrel batch to boil the extract, assuming you have a pot that is large enough.

Klassic Kölsch (All Grain)

This is *the* recipe if you want to make the perfect Kölsch. Using 10% malted wheat and a step-infusion mash, this recipe is guaranteed to please.

Malt	5 Gallons	1 Barrel
Pilsner malt	7 lb. (3.18 kg)	43 lb. (19.52 kg)
Wheat malt	0.75 lb. (0.34 kg)	4.75 lb. (2.16 kg)

Hops	5 Gallons	1 Barrel
Perle (boil begin)	0.44 g alpha acid	2.7 g alpha acid
Perle (40 minutes in)	0.29 g alpha acid	1.8 g alpha acid
Hersbrucker (aroma)	0.2 g alpha acid	1.2 g alpha acid

Kölsch Specifications	5 Gallons	1 Barrel
Mash-in liquor:	2.9 gal.	18.2 gal.
Kölsch yeast:	3.25 oz. (100 ml, liquid)	21 oz. (620 ml, liquid)

OG: 11.3 °P
BU: 22
ADF: 82%

Heat the brewing liquor to 131 °F (55 °C) (or whatever temperature is necessary to hit the strike temperature given your brewery conditions) and mash-in. The desired mashed-in temperature is 117 °F (47 °C). Heat at a rate of two degrees Fahrenheit or one degree Celsius per minute to 143 °F (62 °C). Rest here for 30 minutes and then heat to 159 °F (71 °C). Hold until saccharification is complete (10 to 15 minutes) and then heat to the mash-off temperature of 170 to 173 °F (77 to 78 °C). Transfer to lauter tun and begin vorlauf/recirculation after 10 minutes. Sparge using water that is approximately 170 to 175 °F (77 to 79 °C), or at a temperature where the grain bed is at 170 °F (77 °C). The first runnings should be at about 18 °Plato. When the boil has begun, add the first hop charge. After 40 minutes, add the second hop charge. Add the aroma hops with 10 to 15 minutes left in the boil. Boil for a total of 90 minutes. After the boil is complete, try to separate as much hot trub from the wort as possible, either through sedimentation or whirlpool. Cool wort to 59 °F (15 °C), aerate well, and add yeast. Ferment at 59 to 63 °F (15 to 17 °C). The fermentation should take four to five days before end attenuation is reached. If carbonating using priming sugar or forced carbonation, allow to end ferment. Otherwise, transfer to a pressurized aging vessel with 15% residual fermentable sugar. If possible, cool from 59 to 32 °F (15 to 0 °C) over five to seven days. Allow pressure to build in aging vessel and hold temperature at 32 °F (0 °C) for 21 days. Carbonate to 2.3 volumes for keg Kölsch and 2.5 to 2.65 volumes for bottled Kölsch. Clarify as desired, transfer to bottle or keg, and serve at 46 to 50 °F (8 to 10 °C).

American-Style Kölsch (All Grain)

If you don't have the ability to carry out a step-infusion mash, this is an ideal recipe. This single-temperature infusion mash is done at 145 °F (63 °C), which should result in a dry beer with a high degree of attenuation.

Malt	5 Gallons	1 Barrel
Pilsner malt	8.25 lb. (3.75 kg)	51.125 lb. (26.4 kg)

Hops	5 Gallons	1 Barrel
Hallertau (boil begin)	0.65 g alpha acid	4 g alpha acid
Tettnang		
(30 minutes into boil)	0.32 g alpha acid	2 g alpha acid
Tettnang (aroma)	0.32 g alpha acid	2 g alpha acid

Kölsch Specifications	5 Gallons	1 Barrel
Mash-in liquor:	2.5 gal.	17.4 gal.
Kölsch yeast, liquid:	3.25 oz. (100 ml)	21 oz. (620 ml)

OG: 11.5 °P
BU: 30
ADF: 85%

Heat liquor to 154 °F (68 °C) or to such a temperature that the mash-in temperature is 143 to 148 °F (62 to 64 °C). Allow to convert for one hour. If transferring to lauter tun, let it to settle for 10 minutes before recirculating, otherwise begin vorlauf after one hour. Sparge at 172 °F (78 °C). Add Hallertau hops at beginning of boil, and first charge of Tettnangs 30 minutes into boil. Add aroma hops 15 minutes before the end of the boil. Boil for a total of 90 minutes. Remove hot trub, cool to 64 to 68 °F (18 to 20 °C), and aerate well before adding yeast. Ferment at 64 °F (18 °C) until end attenuation point is reached, or 15% of fermentable sugar remains. Fermentation should take three to four days. Proceed as for the Klassic Kölsch recipe, except carbonate to 2.45 volumes for draft and 2.7 volumes for bottles. Serve at 41 °F (5 °C).

Nineteenth-Century Hop-Bitter Lager Beer (All Grain)

You knew this one had to be coming. As much as you've been teased by all of the discussion of what the Kölsch of yesteryear must have been like, it's time to try it out. This is for hop heads only. This is a multitemperature infusion mash brew, but it can probably be done well as a single-temperature mash also. Because it is so hoppy, and because beers probably didn't have as high an apparent degree of attenuation (ADF) 100 years ago as they do today, we'll shoot for a lower ADF. A long lager time is necessary due to the huge hop rates and because that's how this beer was traditionally aged.

Malt	5 Gallons	1 Barrel
Pilsner malt	5 lb. (2.27 kg)	31 lb. (14.1 kg)
Wheat malt	1 lb. (0.45 kg)	6.2 lb. (2.8 kg)

Hops	5 Gallons	1 Barrel
Perle (first wort)	1.95 g alpha acid	12 g alpha acid
Hallertau (boil begin)	1 g alpha acid	6 g alpha acid
Hersbrucker (aroma)	0.65 g alpha acid	4 g alpha acid

Kölsch Specifications	5 Gallons	1 Barrel
Mash-in liquor:	2.2 gal.	13.5 gal.
Kölsch yeast, liquid:	2.5 oz. (75 ml)	15.5 oz. (465 ml)

OG:	8.5 °P
BU:	60
ADF:	75%

Mash-in at 104 °F (40 °C) and raise temperature to 122 °F (50 °C). Hold for 20 minutes and then heat to 147 °F (64 °C). Hold for 10 minutes and then raise to the saccharification temperature of 159 °F (71 °C). Hold here for 10 minutes and then raise to the mash-off temperature (170 to 173 °F/77 to 78 °C). Transfer to lauter tun, allow to settle for 10 minutes, and then begin recirculation. Add the first hop charge as soon as the first runnings are collected, that is when sparging begins. (Those who are patient enough to read this far into the book, and who are crazy enough to try this recipe, get a little bonus. First wort hopping is a practice that is gaining in popularity again after about an 80-year hiatus. Contrary to what you would think, it actually accentuates the hop aroma and flavor of a beer. I am a big believer in the practice and have obtained great results with it.)

When all the wort is collected and the boil has begun, add the Hallertau hops. Fifteen minutes before the end of the boil, add the Hersbruckers. Boil for 90 minutes.

Remove hot trub, cool to 59 °F (15 °C), and aerate. Ferment at 57 °F (14 °C) (lower if you're feelin' lucky) until end-attenuated or until 15% of fermentable extract remains. Cool to 44 °F (7 °C) and hold for one week, then cool to 35 °F (2 °C) and hold for two months. You may want to fine this beer if you want to brew an unfiltered Kölsch wiess. Carbonate at 2.1 volumes in the keg, 2.4 in bottles. Serve at 50 °F (10 °C) and see how many of your friends will come to your house the next time you invite them back for one of your new creations.

Bonn-Bonn Kölsch (All Grain)

George Fix contributed this recipe, which won a gold medal in the German-style ale category for the American Homebrewers Association's® National Homebrew Competition. Fix's opinion on Kölsch is that "slightly bigger is better."

Malt	5 Gallons	1 Barrel	
German Pils malt	6.25 lb.	39 lb.	
White wheat malt	1.0 lb.	6.75 lb.	
Cara wheat malt	0.75 lb.	4.5 lb.	

Hops	5 Gallons	1 Barrel	% Alpha Acid
German Tettnang	0.5 oz.	3.5 oz.	3
German Hallertau Traditional	0.5 oz.	3.5 oz.	5
German Spält Select	0.5 oz.	3.5 oz.	4

Kölsch

Kölsch Specifications	5 Gallons	1 Barrel
Mash-in liquor:	2.5 gal.	16 gal.
Boiling water:	1.25 gal.	7 gal.
Collect:	5.4 gal.	33.3 gal.
Boil:	10% evaporation to approximately 5 gal.	10% evaporation to approximately 31 gal.

Yeast: White Labs WLP 001 (15 million cells/ml and at least 90% viability)
OG: 12 °P
FG: 2.5 °P
IBU: approximately 25[a]

[a] This measurement is the concentration of iso-alpha-acids mg/l.

Mash-in at 104 °F (40 °C) and hold for 30 minutes. Add boiling water and hold at 140 °F (60 °C) for 30 minutes. Then heat to 158 to 162 °F (70 to 72 °C) and hold for 15 minutes. Collect wort and boil. Ferment at 59 °F (15 °C) for seven days and age three to five weeks at 35 °F (2 °C).

The Breweries of Cologne

At the time this book was written there were 22 brewing companies in Germany that could legally brew Kölsch or have Kölsch contract brewed with their brand names. The listing that follows gives some insight into the history of some of these breweries, what their product mixes are, where they distribute, and whether or not they have a brewpub.

For those of you who can read German, check out the Web site of the Association of Cologne Brewers at http://www.koelner-brauerei-verband.de.

Altstadt-Bräu Joh. Sion KG

Burgmauer 4
50667 Köln
Tel: 0221 96 29 90
Fax: 0221 96 29 91 77

The brewery where Sion Kölsch is brewed has changed hands more times than a rugby ball, but Sion Kölsch is an excellent beer that is well known in Cologne. The brewery's showcase pub in the city center of Cologne is worth a visit. The food is outstanding.

Bergische Löwen Brauerei GmbH & Co. KG
Bergische Gladbach Strasse 116-134
51065 Köln
Tel: 0221 96 29 90
Fax: 0221 96 29 91 77

This brewery is better known for its brand name, Gilden Kölsch. This brand has an appropriate name, even if the German word *gilde* refers more to an organization of businessmen than tradesmen. Like many breweries in Cologne, this one has its roots in the nineteenth century, produced lager beers in the late nineteenth and early twentieth centuries, was destroyed in World War II, and now produces only Kölsch. Today the brewery is controlled by German Brewery Holding, which is a 100% subsidiary of the Brau & Brunnen beverage conglomerate. Unfortunately, you will read these names many times in the pages that follow.

Brauerei Peter Schopen GmbH
Glescher Weg 7
50181 Bedburg

Tel: 022 72 20 08

Fax: 022 72 823 80

Yet another victim of the lawsuits that the Wicküler Brauerei brought against breweries outside Cologne that branded their beers Kölsch, this brewery could not muster the fight to defend its position. Thus, since 1978 Peter Schopen has allowed the Sünner Brauerei in Cologne to brew his Kölsch. The brewery is known for its quality beers, evidenced by the countless medals and certificates of excellence that decorate the company's walls. Today, the Sünner Brauerei contract brews approximately 20,000 hl of Severins Kölsch.

In the nineteenth century the original facility was a brewery, maltery, and distillery all in one. At the time it was operated by the Fassbinder (appropriately known as Cooper in English) family, which was related to the Schopen family. In 1872 Wilhelm Schopen took over the brewery, and since that time it has been under family control.

Brauerei zur Malzmühle Schwartz KG

Heumarkt 6

50667 Köln

Tel: 0221 21 01 18

Fax: 0221 24 77 01

Located near the Rhein in the center of the city, the Malzmühle (malt mill) is a cornerstone of the Heumarkt (haymarket) Square in Cologne. The Heumarkt was one of the largest markets in the city. "Travelers in the Middle Ages praised its beauty and magnificence" (Mathar/Spiegel 1989, 81). The Heumarkt has been the location of many important buildings in Cologne's history, such as the slaughterhouse, the commodities exchange, and the theater. The Heumarkt has also been an important place for the brewers of Cologne throughout the centuries. The town malt mill was located here from 1572 to 1853 (hence the name Brauerei zur Malzmühle). The Heumarkt was also home to the grain scales and the coopers whose guild house was right around the corner.

The first mention of Haus number 6 is documented in 1165, but it wasn't until 1858 that the brewer Hubert Koch founded the brewery. The Koch family also produced malt extract, and the full name of the company by 1912 was Jakob Koch, Bier- und Malzextrakt-Dampfbrauerei. Today the Schwarz family upholds the tradition of brewing at the

Heumarkt. The brewery produces approximately 50,000 hl a year for sale in the brewery's pub and in Cologne. More than 75% of the beer brewed at Malzmühle ends up in kegs. The beer at the Malzmühle is outstanding, with a bit fuller body and mouthfeel than many Kölsch beers.

The brewery's pub is a must-see in Cologne. The Malzmühle typifies the bustle of a Cologne pub, and I can remember being there one time with a group of eight, when our Köbes filled the circumference of two beer coasters with marks indicating the number of beers we had ordered. The authenticity of the pub is highlighted by its beichtstuhl and unique accounting system. The Köbesse all purchase tokens at the beginning of their shifts, and each time they order beers they must pay for them at the bar right away with the tokens. The food at the Malzmühle is also excellent.

Brauhaus zur Garde AG

Neusser Strasse 617
50737 Köln
Tel: 0221 33 508 20
Fax: 0221 33 508 70

I wasn't able to ascertain the exact date this brewery was founded, but it was sometime in the late nineteenth century. The brewery used to be called the Dormagener

Brewery and was purchased around the turn of the century by Heinrich Becker (see the entry for Privatbrauerei Gaffel Becker). At some point in the first half of the twentieth century, the brewery was sold to the Dortmunder Aktienbrauerei (DAB) but was still branded as Dormagener Kölsch. In 1966 the brewery was sold to the Harzheim family and has been in their hands ever since.

Initially Dormagener Kölsch was rebranded Kess Kölsch, but since 1979 the beer produced from this facility has been known as Garde Kölsch. Today the brewery produces about 100,000 hl of beer with 35 employees. The ratio of keg to bottle product is about 60:40. Garde Kölsch is sold within about a 100-kilometer radius of the brewery. In 1976 the family purchased the Bürger brewery and production of Bürger Kölsch was moved to the brewery in Dormagen (see the entry for Rheinische Bürger Bräu).

Cölner Hofbräu P. Josef Früh, Köln

Am Hof 12-14

50667 Köln

Tel: 0221 2 58 03 94

Founded in 1904 by Peter Josef Früh, this brewery has been characterized by one success story after another. Früh had actually purchased another brewery in 1895 in Cologne, but sold it in 1898. Early on Früh differentiated himself from his competitors by having a brewpub with the brewery and by brewing a beer that was sensorially unique. It is speculated that Früh was one of the first breweries in Cologne to take advantage of filtration technology by producing a clear beer. Früh also backed off on the hops a little bit, and so his beer was arguably a transition from the hop-bitter lager beer of the nineteenth century to the Kölsch that is now produced in Cologne.

Even today, Früh is known as one of the palest of the Kölsch beers.

The brewery had traditionally been more of a brewpub, but in the 1960s Früh started to challenge the other breweries in Cologne as the top producer of Kölsch. In 1969 Früh Kölsch became available in bottles, and by 1976 the brewery was selling almost 100,000 hl per year. Currently the brewery annually produces around 400,000 hl under the Früh label, including an alcohol-free Kölsch. The brewery is still under family control, and all of the production is sold within a 200-kilometer radius of the brewery.

Although Früh is now brewed outside the downtown area of Cologne, the brewery still has two of the most famous pubs in Cologne, Früh am Dom and Früh im Veedel.

Dom-Brauerei GmbH

Tacitussstrasse 15
50968 Köln (Bayenthal)
Telephone: 0221 3 76 08-0
Fax: 0221 3 76 08-11

Dom is the German word for "cathedral," and the Dom brewery is fortunate enough to have *the* landmark of Cologne as its logo. The origins of the Dom-Brauerei go back to 1894 when the brothers Steingröver took over two brewpubs belonging to Carl Göter. After the merger, the new brewery was called Hirsch Brauerei Goeter & Steingröver. The brothers Steingröver also purchased 130,000 square feet of land for future expansion. As the expansion was underway a tornado hit the brew house in 1898 and severely damaged it.

Like many Cologne breweries at the time, the Hirsch Brauerei had a brewing operation in the nearby Eifel region of Germany on the shores of a lake. The reason: access to ice. Refrigeration machines weren't quite economical enough at the time, and breweries used ice to keep beer cool. As nearly all breweries had done for centuries, blocks of ice were removed from frozen lakes, transported to the breweries, then stored in subterranean, stone-walled cellars for use during the brewing year. In the late nineteenth century the blocks of ice were transported to the Hirsch Brauerei by train. The brewery, like many at the time, delivered ice blocks to customers using horse-drawn wagons.

In 1900 the Hirsch Brauerei became a public company and in the years that followed the company acquired smaller breweries in and around Cologne. At the turn of the century the brewery produced lagers under the names Hirsch Gold Export and Hirsch Edel Pils. Hirsch Beer was also bottled for the first time around 1900.

The brewery merged with the Adler-Brauerei of Cologne in 1931, and the name of the new company was Adler- und Hirsch Brauerei. Even before World War II, the terror of the Hitler regime affected the breweries of Cologne. In the name of aryanizing Germany, the main shareholders of the brewery were forced to give up their interest because they were Jewish. Even "Hirsch" had to be removed from the brewery name. The founding families of the Essener Aktien-Brauerei acquired the majority stake in the brewery.

After the brewery was bombed out in World War II, production resumed, but most of the output was allocated to the occupying British troops. By 1957 production was up to 100,000 hl, most of which was Dom Kölsch. Beginning in 1965, the brewery began investing heavily in improved technology and increased capacity. After merging with the Hitdorfer Brauerei, the Dom-Brauerei was acquired in 1972 by the Stern-Brauerei Carl Funke in Essen. In 1974 production of lager beer shifted to Essen, and since that time only top-fermented Kölsch is brewed at the Dom-Brauerei.

Today Dom is one of the largest Kölsch breweries, producing more than 400,000 hl in 1997. Although Kölsch is a specialty of Cologne, Dom is widely available all over Germany, in some cases even on tap. Like most Kölsch breweries, Dom produces more beer to be sold in kegs than bottles. Their Kölsch is available in a variety of packages, including one-half-liter bottles, six packs of 33-centiliter bottles, cans, and kegs. The brewery recently introduced Dom Pils into the market in an effort to leverage the existing brand strength, capitalize on the growth of the Pils category, and capture some of the younger consumer segment. (Kölsch is a more "traditional" beer style, and heaven forbid that the youth of Germany be caught drinking the more traditional beverages.) Dom has also introduced a superpremium positioned Kölsch for those places where haute cuisine is served.

Erzquell-Brauerei Bielstein Haas & Co. KG

Bielsteiner Strasse 108

51674 Wiehl-Bielstein

Tel: 022 62 8 20

Fax: 022 62 8 21 06

This brewery is much better known for its Zunft (which means guild) Kölsch than by the name of the brewery itself. Located in Bielstein, it is the easternmost of the 22 Kölsch breweries. The brand has existed since the 1950s, but the brewery was founded around the turn of the century as the Adler Brauerei. The founder, Ernst Kindl, was involved in textiles, but as the margins in that business began to deteriorate, he decided to pursue another career. His beer gained in popularity in the hilly area east of Cologne. In the early 1930s the brewery was renamed the Bielsteiner Brauerei and it also bought a majority interest in the Siegtal brewery. In 1976 the fusion of the two companies was complete, and today 200,000 hl of Zunft Kölsch are brewed at the brewery in Bielstein, and Pils is produced at the brewery in Siegen. The brewery in Bielstein produces about 40% keg beer and 60% bottled beer. The region where the brewery is located is well known for its spring water, and the brewery proudly claims on its label that Zunft Kölsch is "brewed with crystal-clear, soft water from our own spring."

Ganser Brauerei GmbH & Co. KG

Birkengartenstrasse 7

51373 Leverkusen

Tel: 02 14 38 80

Fax: 02 14 38 880

This is another brewery that is located outside the city limits of Cologne, in the nearby city of Leverkusen. Founded in 1879 by Peter Ganser, the brewery quickly gained a reputation for quality, underscored by the fact that the beer was awarded the prestigious gold medal at the 1900 fair in Strassburg. The original brewery was actually built in the city of Lechenich, which today is a part of the town of Erftstadt. In 1910 the Ganser family purchased a brewery in Leverkusen as a second production facility. After World War I, all of the brewing was shifted to Leverkusen. Prior to World War II, the brewery reached a production peak of 22,000 hl.

Today, under the leadership of the family's fourth generation, the brewery is producing approximately 150,000 hl annually. Sixty-five employees help brew and sell Ganser Kölsch, which is sold almost exclusively within the Kölsch region. Primary fermentation occurs in open fermenters, and aging takes place in giant, cylindro-conical tanks. The percentage of keg to bottle beer produced is about 58:42. In addition to the Ganser Kölsch, the brewery also produces Ganser Kölsch Light, Ganser Kölsch Zero (my guess is this would be the alcohol-free version), and a bock beer called Ganserator.

Gebrüder Sünner GmbH & Co. KG

Kalker Hauptstrasse 260

51103 Köln

Tel: 0221 98 79 90

Fax: 0221 87 83 81

Christian Sünner bought the Zum Schiffgen Brewery in 1846. Located on the east bank of the Rhein, the complex was a brewery, distillery, and pub all rolled into one. As the brewery grew in the nineteenth century, it embraced all of the techniques and engineering advances that modern brewing has become known for, including lager beer production. The brewery is actually credited with being the first to brew a Bavarian-style lager in Cologne. By the 1920s the brewery had bock, export, Märzen, and Pilsner styles in its product mix. Its Kölsch had been a part of the product family since 1906, and in 1918 the term *Kölsch* was used to describe the top-fermenting beer. Indeed, this may have been the first time that Kölsch was used to reference the style that was hopbitter lager beer. The brewery suffered the same fate that most of Cologne's breweries did in World War II, but today the brewery is prospering with 60 employees and an annual production of 60,000 hl.

Giesler Brauerei GmbH & Co.
Uhlstrasse 96
50321 Brühl
Tel: 022 32 94 51 00
Fax: 022 32 94 510 33

The original brewery site was first documented in 1852, but it wasn't until 1874 that Friedrich Giesler purchased the brewery, which had had many owners. Like many breweries in the late nineteenth century, the Giesler Brauerei enjoyed rapid growth until World War I. In 1917 the brewery merged with the Schlossbrauerei Brühl AG and formed the Brühler Brauerei-Gesellschaften GmbH. The hard work of the Giesler family and the reputation the brewery's products had in the marketplace led to the renaming of the merged company back to Giesler in 1925.

Shortly after World War II, the brewery's own well supplied the residents of Brühl with water, because the public supply system was damaged. In 1953 Giesler Kölsch was released on the market. Today the brewery produces approximately 70,000 hl of beer, using open fermenters and closed, cylindro-conical aging tanks. In addition to the Giesler Kölsch, which constitutes about

90% of the brewery's sales, the brewery produces Giesler Alt and a Pilsner. The brewery also produces a light beer with a lager yeast called Brühler Leicht. Like so many of the other Kölsch producers, the brewery kegs more than 70% of its product. The brewery also contract brews Schreckenskammer Kölsch.

Küppers Brauerei GmbH & Co. KG
Alteburger Strasse 145-155
50968 Köln
Tel: 0221 3 77 90
Fax: 0221 9 62 990

The location of the brewery was originally a warehouse for the Wicküler-Küpper Brauerei AG, located in Elberfeld. The warehouse was a distribution terminal for the Pilsner and export beer that the brewery was selling in Cologne. Right before World War II, a large expansion was supposed to take place, but the war put the construction plans on hold. In the early 1960s the brewery recognized an emerging market for Kölsch, so Küppers Kölsch made an entrance into the Cologne beer market in 1962, and was an overnight success.

In 1964 the first test brew was completed at the company's own facility, and there has been no looking back ever since. Today the brewery has a capacity of 1.4 million hl and distributes the product throughout Germany and internationally. At one point the Dutch brewer Grolsch actually owned Wicküler, and thus Küppers, but in 1994 German Brewery Holding overtook the leadership of the company.

Kurfürsten-Bräu GmbH

Bornheimer Str. 42-52

53111 Bonn

Tel: 02 28 51 00

Fax: 02 28 51 02 77

Located in the capital city of the former West Germany, this brewery has a very long and dynamic history. Originally founded in 1385, the brewery now contract brews its products at its sister brewery in Cologne, Gilden Kölsch Brauerei. World War II arguably had the greatest impact on the history of the brewery. Difficulty in obtaining raw materials at the end of the war led to the brewery's lowest production. The brewery facility was also so badly damaged that complete reconstruction was necessary. Unable to rebuild the brewery with their own means, the owners of the brewery sold the majority interest to the Dortmunder Union-Brauerei in 1950. At that time, the brewery was also renamed Kurfürsten-Bräu AG. Over the next few decades, production at the brewery grew rapidly, from 15,000 hl to a high of

250,000 hl in 1980. By 1992, however, production had dropped to 157,000 hl, and in 1993 the brewery was sold to German Brewery Holding. There are actually two different Kölsch products available from this company: Kurfürsten Kölsch and Kurfürsten Maximilian Kölsch. The latter has carved out a bit of a niche for itself by being the only Kölsch available in swing top bottles.

Monheimer Brauerei Peters & Bambeck

Krummstrasse 30

40789 Monheim

Tel: 0 21 73 955 50

Fax: 0 21 73 95 55 55

Being located at the northern border of Kölsch country, it is not surprising that this brewery also produces alt. What is interesting is that this relatively small brewery (30,000 hl per year) also produces a wheat beer, a Pilsner, a *festbier,* and an alcohol-free beer. Ninety-five percent of the brewery's Kölsch production is in kegs, which is often a strong testament to a brewery's local, if not cult, following. Most of the brewery's production ends up in Köln, Düsseldorf, and Wuppertal. The brewery also opened an outlet for its products in 1994 in Cologne. Appropriately the brewery's pub is located on the grounds of the once-famous brewpub, Zum Kranz.

The brewery has always been in the Peters family, which has also dabbled in malting and sauerkraut production. Like many brewpubs in the nineteenth century, the Peters's brewery recognized an opportunity to sell beer away from the pub and expanded the brewing facility to satisfy the growing demand. The brewery also hopped on the lager bandwagon and produced bottom-fermented beers. The brewery came out of World War II relatively unscathed. Perhaps this is why the brewery has been able to stay under family control, unlike so many other Kölsch breweries. In fact, the brewery has been so successful that it has made major improvements to the brewery in the 1990s: a new fermentation and aging cellar in 1993 and a new brew house in 1996.

Obergärige Hausbrauerei Päffgen

Friesenstrasse 64-66

50670 Köln

Tel: 0221 13 54 61

Fax: 0221 13 92 005

This is the type of brewpub that oozes tradition and smacks of authenticity. Complete with beichtstuhl, Köbes, and a gravity-dispensing, wooden cask, this is a must-see pub for anyone embarking on a Kölsch pilgrimage. Like many older generation urban brewpubs in Germany, the Päffgen brewery is in the rear of the building in the courtyard area of the lot. Originally founded in 1883 by Hermann Päffgen, the brewery was first located at Friesenstrasse 64, but the 66 location was annexed in the 1930s. The location of the current bar was at one time the street entrance for the horse-drawn beer wagons parked in the courtyard.

The beer at Päffgen is as good as Kölsch gets. Dispensed from wooden casks that are placed atop the bar, the beer has a delicate carbonation that can only come from beer served this way. Although it has been several years since I have been fortunate enough to drink a Päffgen Kölsch, I remember the beer being very soft and well balanced with a pleasant ester character that was unique among the Kölsch beers. This beer has made huge deposits into the karma bank of brewing. Päffgen Kölsch is brewed in copper kettles, fermented in open fermenters, hand-filled into wooden barrels, and available only on draft. It is the smallest of all of the Kölsch breweries (6,000 hl per year), and in this case, size doesn't matter. If you have time to see only one brewery or brewpub while in Cologne, make it Päffgen.

Privatbrauerei Gaffel Becker & Co.

Eigelstein 41

50668 Köln

Tel: 0221 160 06 10

Fax: 0221 13 31 07

E-mail: gaffel@netcologne.de

Web site: http://www.gaffel.de/pbrau1.html

Brewery's pub: Gaffel-Haus

Alter Markt 20

50667 Köln

Open from 11 A.M. to 12:45 A.M. every day

According to management at the brewery, the first official mention of Gaffel-Haus is in 1302. In 1908 the Becker family took over the brewery. Today the brewery produces approximately 360,000 hl of Kölsch each year. In addition to the Gaffel-Kölsch Classic, the brewery also produces a light Kölsch and an alcohol-free Kölsch. The Classic is very representative of the style, with a starting gravity of approximately 11.3 °Plato and bitterness of 25 IBU. The light has a reduced alcohol content of 2.5% by volume. (In Germany the concept of light beer applies more to alcohol than to calories. In Germany, and Europe on the whole, allowable blood alcohol levels when driving are lower, so light beers were developed as a means to still be able to have a few rounds without having to worry about driving under the influence.) The starting gravity of the light is about 7.5% (Germany has certain original gravity classes into which all beer must fall. Normal or vollbier is 11 to 14 °Plato, bock beer is more than 16 °Plato, and the original gravity of schank beer must fall between 7 and 8 °Plato. Beers with starting gravities between these categories are called gap beers and are illegal to brew.) The Gaffel Frei alcohol-free Kölsch has less alcohol than a glass of orange juice.

The brewery still produces some of its beer in open fermenters and horizontal aging tanks. Recent expansions have gone hand in hand with the implementation of modern cylindro-conical fermenters. Gaffel Kölsch can be packaged in anything from a 33-centiliter bottle to multi-hectoliter tanks on wheels for dispensing at large events. Approximately 90% of the brewery's beer is sold within a 100-kilometer radius of the brewery, but if you are in Spain, Italy, or Florida, you might be lucky enough to find a cold Gaffel Kölsch.

The brewery also has a pub, Zur Bretzel, on Alter Markt 20-22. This is one of the older buildings in

Cologne, and its first mention dates back to 1215. The building used to be called Zur Britzele am Apfelmarkt because it was right in front of the open air market, where apparently many apples were sold. The building lasted for the better part of 700 years before it underwent a major restoration from 1910 to 1912. Unfortunately the new and improved building didn't last nearly as long, as it was completely destroyed in World War II. The building was completely reconstructed in 1955 and is now the showpiece pub for the Privatbrauerei Gaffel.

Privat-Brauerei Heinrich Reissdorf GmbH & Co.
Severinstrasse 51
50678 Köln
Tel: 0221 31 60 51
Fax: 0221 31 15 71

Located in the heart of Cologne and rich in history, this brewery just celebrated its 100th anniversary in 1994. At age 50, Heinrich Reissdorf started the brewery on the advice of his sons. A successful tailor, Reissdorf was apparently looking for a new challenge in life. He died seven years after starting the brewery, but his wife and five sons continued his work. In 1923 the brewery added bottom-fermenting beers to its palette of styles. In 1936 Reissdorf was the first brewery in Cologne to bottle Kölsch. On

March 2, 1945, the brewery was completely flattened by a bomb attack. Carl Reissdorf, one of the operating owners, was killed on the last day of the war.

After the war, the family began to pick up the pieces and rebuild the brewery. The brewery's well helped to supply the neighborhood with water. By 1948 the brewery produced beer again, albeit a very simple beer with a starting gravity of only 4 °Plato. Within the next couple of years the brewery was producing a lager beer, a Pilsner, an export, and a dark beer, all in addition to the Kölsch. Since the beginning of the 1970s, the brewery has exclusively produced Kölsch. Today, under the direction of the fourth generation of brewing Reissdorfs, the brewery employs about 80 people and produces around 300,000 hl per year. Because the brewery is located in the center of Cologne, further expansion has been difficult, so the brewery is doing some off-site bottling and warehousing. Reissdorf Kölsch is very true to style: very pale, very well attenuated, moderately hopped, and extremely drinkable!

Privatbrauerei Robert Metzmacher KG

Tacitusstrasse 15

50968 Köln

Tel: 0221 37 60 80

Fax: 0221 37 60 811

Brewing rights were granted to the Metzmacher family in 1723, and for the next 150 years the brewery was operated as a brewpub. In 1879 Robert Metzmacher took over the brewery and scaled up production to be able to distribute beer. Metzmacher took advantage of late nineteenth-century brewing technology by purchasing a steam boiler to heat his brew kettle and refrigeration equipment to be able to produce his lager beer, Johannis-Bräu.

After World War II, the brewery was one of the few authorized to brew for the English troops occupying Cologne. At the time, the beer is said to have had a starting gravity of around 8 °Plato and an alcohol content of 2.6% by volume, which was about as strong a beer as was available at the time! Since 1955, the brewery has produced Rats-Kölsch, which has nothing to do with black rodents that have long tails. This name has a meaning that is more like "the beer of the (city) council," much like the Ratskeller, where the city council would likely be found drinking the Rats-Kölsch. In 1975 the brewery stopped making other beers, such as the Johannis Pils, and today approximately 50,000 hl per year of Rats-Kölsch are brewed. Like many other breweries in Cologne and Germany, the brewery was recently absorbed by the Dom-Brauerei. Rats-Kölsch still has a loyal following because it is a little bit darker and hoppier than most other Kölsch beers.

Privatbrauerei Sester GmbH & Co. KG
Mündelstrasse 35-41
51065 Köln
Tel: 0221 9 62 04 0
Fax: 0221 9 62 04 333

The brewery's older history is probably more interesting than its more recent one. The brewery has existed since 1805, and it was taken over by the Sester brothers in 1902. In 1918 the brothers purchased the shares that another brewery owned of the Kölner Brauhaus Vereinsbrauerei, or United Cologne Brewery. The history of this brewery dates back to 1896, but the key date for this alliance of brewers was 1904 when the brewery was sold to various publicans in Cologne. The idea was to unify under this brewery to ward off the onslaught of beers being shipped into Cologne from Bavaria and the nearby Ruhrgebiet. The brewery apparently had enjoyed moderate success, but material shortages in World War I forced it to close. The Sester Brauerei continued to grow and expand until World War II. In fact, in 1928 the Sester Brauerei acquired another brewery. World War II destroyed both breweries, and after the war, reconstruction occurred only at the original brewery site. Unfortunately, the brewery was destroyed again, this time a victim of the beer wars. Sester Kölsch is now contract brewed, and the company is controlled by the gigantic German beverage conglomerate, Brau & Brunnen. The brewery was torn down in 1995, and Sester Kölsch is now available only in bottles.

Rheinische Bürger Bräu GmbH & Co. KG
Neusser Strasse 617
50737 Köln
Tel: 0221 7 40 90 91
Fax: 0221 74 43 03

The youngest of the 22 member breweries belonging to the Kölsch Konvention, Bürger Kölsch first came to market in 1966. The brewery was actually the Steffens Brauerei, which had been producing bottom-fermenting beers since the nineteenth century. The Dortmunder Hansa Brauerei bought this regional brewery, renamed it the Rheinische Bürger Brauerei, and then it began producing Kölsch. The brewery became embroiled in a suit regarding the company's use of "Kölsch" to brand its product (the brewery was located in Euskirchen, which was on the outskirts of Kölsch country), and eventually the legal fees proved to be too much to bear. At the same time the brewery was sold to the Dortmunder Aktien Brauerei. In 1973 the Harzheim family purchased the brewery (see the entry for Brauhaus zur Garde) and all of the production was transferred to Dormagen in Cologne. Bürger Kölsch is available only in bottles, and production is less than 20,000 hl.

Richmodis-Bräu vorm. Brauhaus Friedrich Winter

Welserstrasse 16

51149 Köln

Tel: 0 22 03 93 39 42

Fax: 0 22 03 93 39 49

The name Richmodis comes from an old legend in Cologne. A woman named Richmodis was apparently falsely diagnosed with the plague and was buried alive, since she was presumed dead. Remarkably, she escaped from her coffin. A more appropriate story to describe the history of this brewery would be the one about the cat with nine lives.

Friedrich Winter came to Cologne in 1874 and leased the Ursulabräu. In 1877 he bought a pub and a lager cellar.

He became a pioneer of modern brewing, reflected in part by his desire to brew more than just the traditional top-fermented styles. He brewed Winter Pilsener, Winter Münchener, and even a Winter Doppel-Märzen. I don't know if I'm familiar with that style, but it sure sounds good. It wasn't until 1930 that the Winter family bought the Richmodis-Bräu. The family decided to sell the brewery in 1968, and it has since been bought and sold two more times. Just this year it was sold to the Gaffel Brauerei in Cologne. Despite its many owners in recent years, the brewery still enjoys a strong reputation as a brewer of high-quality Kölsch. The brewery produces about 90,000 hl per year, about 90% of which is packaged in kegs.

Cologne's Classic Cuisine

Like much of Germany's cuisine, Cologne's is tradi-tionally hearty and nourishing. Cologne is in the Catholic part of Germany, and so on Fridays dried cod was the dish of choice for the midday meal. For dinner the leftover fish was mixed with potatoes, onions, milk, and butter into *kuschelemusch*. Canned vegetables, like green beans, cabbage, and beet stalks, were a winter favorite, as well as pickled meat. Also, the beer of Cologne has always been an important part of mealtime. Fifty years ago in the evening the streets were filled with the cacophony of con-versation and clanging metal as the youth went to the local brewery to pick up a pail full of beer for dinner.

A menu in a Cologne pub is called a *foderkaat,* and is true to the traditional hearty cuisine of Cologne. One of the most famous and most simple specialties of Cologne is the *halver hahn,* or half rooster. It is nothing more than a thick slice of medium-aged Dutch cheese on a rye roll.

Some of the older specialties that have disappeared from the Kölsch menu are: *bierzupp* (fairly obvious), *botter-milch-bunne-zupp* (buttermilk bean soup), *sorekappeszupp* (sauerkraut soup), and *jestuvte murre met brodwoosch* (braised carrots with bratwurst). Of course, for the gourmet there is always Kölsch caviar, which is "nothing other than blood sausage that is fried so long in a pan that it turns into a bunch of dark crumbs that aren't dissimilar to Sturgeon eggs" (Mathar/Spiegel 1989, 158).

Some of the most popular and traditional dishes of Cologne are what follows. For the curious culinarian there are even time-tested recipes to try out on your willing neighbors and friends. For the world traveler these dishes are what to look for on your next trip to Cologne.

Klatschkies Met Oellich

This is a very simple recipe, but one requiring good technique and years of experience to be made properly. Soft curd cheese is mixed with the right proportion of evaporated milk until a thick, creamy mixture is obtained. Seasonings include salt, pepper, a pinch of nutmeg, chives, and diced onions. Variations of this recipe include seasoning with paprika or curry. Klatschkies is usually garnished with thin rings of spring onions and then spread on dark bread or onion bread. It is highly recommended to first spread a little butter on the bread to "round out the flavor." Klatschkies also goes well with potatoes. This is obviously not a dish for the cholesterol conscious!

Rievkooche

This dish is typical of the Rheinland, but has cousins that can be found throughout Germany. Essentially, Rievkooche is a very tasty variation on the potato cake/hash brown theme. Although the preparation of Rievkooche is not the simplest, the results are guaranteed to please. To make Rievkooche use the following recipe:

4–5 pounds potatoes, grated
2 onions
1/2 pound bacon fat
2 eggs
salt and pepper to taste

Peel, wash, and coarsely grate the potatoes. Remove as much moisture as possible by drying the grated spuds in a clean cloth or paper towel. Peel and dice the onions. Cut the bacon fat into small cubes. Combine the potatoes, onions, bacon fat, and eggs and season with salt and pepper. Form small cakes and fry in oil or butter until golden brown on both sides. Rievkooche is often served in Cologne with applesauce or a variation of tartar sauce.

Soorbrode

Soorbrode is the Kölsch word for what is perhaps the best known German dish in America: *sauerbraten*. In Germany there are as many variations of sauerbraten from household to household as there are for meatloaf in the United States, but here is one that comes straight from Cologne:

> 2 cups wine vinegar
>
> 4 cups water
>
> 2 bay leaves
>
> cloves
>
> mustard seed
>
> 2–3 peppercorns
>
> 2 juniper berries
>
> 1 teaspoon salt
>
> 1/2 teaspoon pepper
>
> 2 onions, sliced
>
> 2 pounds lean beef (roast)
>
> 3 tablespoons bacon fat
>
> 1/4 cup raisins
>
> 1 teaspoon each of red wine, apple kraut, tomato paste, and sugar

Bring the vinegar and water to a boil and add the spices and onions. Let cool and then cover the meat in an earthen pot and let marinate for two to three days. Take the meat out and dry it. Rub the roast with salt and pepper. Sear in a roasting pan all around with the bacon fat. Strain the marinade and pour the juice over the meat and roast for two hours. Rotate periodically and add a bit of water. Remove the roast from the pan and keep warm. Cook the drippings with the raisins and thicken the gravy to your liking. Sweeten with the sugar if desired and add the red wine, tomato paste, and apple kraut. Serve with applesauce and potato dumplings.

Himmel un Aed (Heaven and Earth)

This is a simple yet refined dish that is sweet and tangy. The three main ingredients are apples, potatoes, and blood sausage (Flönz). The recipe for four people is:

2–2 1/2 pounds potatoes, peeled
5 large apples (Boskop if possible)
1 tablespoon sugar
1 tablespoon lemon juice
1/8 pound smoked bacon or ham
1 pound onions
1/4 cup milk
1 tablespoon butter

salt to taste

nutmeg

1 pound blood sausage

Parboil the peeled potatoes in salted water. Peel the apples, quarter, remove the seeds, and cook over low heat with the sugar and lemon juice to make applesauce. Dice the bacon and cook in a skillet. Slice the onions and cook with the bacon until golden brown. Mash the potatoes and in a separate pan heat the milk, butter, salt, and a pinch of nutmeg. Pour over the potatoes and then whip to a pureed consistency. Mix in the applesauce. Remove the bacon and onions from the skillet and keep warm. Quickly cut the blood sausage into slices about 3/8-inch thick and fry for approximately one minute on each side. Spread the mash on a plate, lay the fried blood sausage slices on top, then garnish with the bacon and onions.

Muuzemandeln

In the Rheinland during Fasching, sweet almonds are a particularly enjoyable treat. The custom of eating almonds during this event is an old one. Before Lent, people loaded up on calories, and as you will see Muuzemandeln isn't for weight watchers.

1/8 pound butter

1/4 pound powdered sugar

2 eggs

2 tablespoons amaretto liqueur

2/3 pound flour

1/4 pound crushed almonds

1 teaspoon baking powder

Soften the butter. Slowly fold in the sugar, eggs, and amaretto. Mix the flour with the baking powder. Stir half of the flour mixture into the liquid mixture and knead in the other half to form a dough. Mix in the crushed almonds and then roll the dough until it is 2 to 3 millimeters thick. Use a cookie cutter to cut out forms and then fry them in hot oil until light brown. Let the oil drain off and then sprinkle with powdered sugar.

Unit Conversion Chart

Index	lb. to kg	oz. to g	fl. oz. to ml
0.25	0.11	7	7
0.50	0.23	14	15
0.75	0.34	21	22
1.00	0.45	28	30
1.25	0.57	35	37
1.50	0.68	43	44
1.75	0.79	50	52
2.00	0.91	57	59
2.25	1.02	64	67
2.50	1.13	71	74
2.75	1.25	78	81
3.00	1.36	85	89
3.25	1.47	92	96
3.50	1.59	99	103
3.75	1.70	106	111
4.00	1.81	113	118
4.25	1.93	120	126
4.50	2.04	128	133
4.75	2.15	135	140
5.00	2.27	142	148
5.25	2.38	149	155
5.50	2.49	156	163
5.75	2.61	163	170
6.00	2.72	170	177
6.25	2.84	177	185
6.50	2.95	184	192
6.75	3.06	191	200
7.00	3.18	198	207
7.25	3.29	206	214
7.50	3.40	213	222
7.75	3.52	220	229
8.00	3.63	227	237
8.25	3.74	234	244
8.50	3.86	241	251
8.75	3.97	248	259
9.00	4.08	255	266
9.25	4.20	262	274
9.50	4.31	269	281
9.75	4.42	276	288
10.00	4.54	283	296
10.25	4.65	291	303
10.50	4.76	298	310
10.75	4.88	305	318
11.00	4.99	312	325
11.25	5.10	319	333
11.50	5.22	326	340
11.75	5.33	333	347
12.00	5.44	340	355

By Philip W. Fleming and Joachim Schüring. Reprinted with permission from *Zymurgy*®.

gal. to l		qt. to l		pt. to l		tsp.	tbsp.	cup
US	UK	US	UK	US	UK	to ml	to ml	to ml
0.95	1.14	0.24	0.28	0.12	0.14	1.2	3.7	59
1.89	2.27	0.47	0.57	0.24	0.28	2.5	7.4	118
2.84	3.41	0.71	0.85	0.35	0.43	3.7	11.1	177
3.79	4.55	0.95	1.14	0.47	0.57	4.9	14.8	237
4.73	5.68	1.18	1.42	0.59	0.71	6.2	18.5	296
5.68	6.82	1.42	1.70	0.71	0.85	7.4	22.2	355
6.62	7.96	1.66	1.99	0.83	0.99	8.6	25.9	414
7.57	9.09	1.89	2.27	0.95	1.14	9.9	29.6	473
8.52	10.23	2.13	2.56	1.06	1.28	11.1	33.3	532
9.46	11.36	2.37	2.84	1.18	1.42	12.3	37.0	591
10.41	12.50	2.60	3.13	1.30	1.56	13.6	40.2	651
11.36	13.64	2.84	3.41	1.42	1.70	14.8	44.4	710
12.30	14.77	3.08	3.69	1.54	1.85	16.0	48.1	769
13.25	15.91	3.31	3.98	1.66	1.99	17.3	51.8	828
14.19	17.05	3.55	4.26	1.77	2.13	18.5	55.4	887
15.14	18.18	3.79	4.55	1.89	2.27	19.7	59.1	946
16.09	19.32	4.02	4.83	2.01	2.42	20.9	62.8	1,005
17.03	20.46	4.26	5.11	2.13	2.56	22.2	66.5	1,065
17.98	21.59	4.50	5.40	2.25	2.70	23.4	70.2	1,124
18.93	22.73	4.73	5.68	2.37	2.84	24.6	73.9	1,183
19.87	23.87	4.97	5.97	2.48	2.98	25.9	77.6	1,242
20.82	25.00	5.20	6.25	2.60	3.13	27.1	81.3	1,301
21.77	26.14	5.44	6.53	2.72	3.27	28.3	85.0	1,360
22.71	27.28	5.68	6.82	2.84	3.41	29.6	88.7	1,419
23.66	28.41	5.91	7.10	2.96	3.55	30.8	92.4	1,479
24.60	29.55	6.15	7.39	3.08	3.69	32.0	96.1	1,538
25.55	30.69	6.39	7.67	3.19	3.84	33.3	99.8	1,597
26.50	31.82	6.62	7.96	3.31	3.98	34.5	103.5	1,656
27.44	32.96	6.86	8.24	3.43	4.12	35.7	107.2	1,715
28.39	34.09	7.10	8.52	3.55	4.26	37.0	110.9	1,774
29.34	35.23	7.33	8.81	3.67	4.40	38.2	114.6	1,834
30.28	36.37	7.57	9.09	3.79	4.55	39.4	118.3	1,893
31.23	37.50	7.81	9.38	3.90	4.69	40.7	122.0	1,952
32.18	38.64	8.04	9.66	4.02	4.83	41.9	125.7	2,011
33.12	39.78	8.28	9.94	4.14	4.97	43.1	129.4	2,070
34.07	40.91	8.52	10.23	4.26	5.11	44.4	133.1	2,129
35.01	42.05	8.75	10.51	4.38	5.26	45.6	136.8	2,188
36.96	43.19	9.99	10.80	4.50	5.40	46.8	140.5	2,248
37.91	44.32	9.23	11.08	4.61	5.54	48.1	144.2	2,307
37.85	45.46	9.46	11.36	4.73	5.68	49.3	147.9	2,366
38.80	46.60	9.70	11.65	4.85	5.82	50.5	151.6	2,425
39.75	47.73	9.94	11.93	4.97	5.97	51.8	155.3	2,484
40.69	48.87	10.17	12.22	5.09	6.11	53.0	159.0	2,543
41.64	50.01	10.41	12.50	5.20	6.25	54.2	162.6	2,602
42.58	51.14	10.65	12.79	5.32	6.39	55.4	166.3	2,662
43.53	52.28	10.88	13.07	5.44	6.53	56.7	170.0	2,721
44.48	53.41	11.12	13.35	5.56	6.68	57.9	173.7	2,780
45.42	54.55	11.36	13.64	5.68	6.82	59.1	177.4	2,839

Glossary

aerate. To force atmospheric air or oxygen into solution. Introduce air to the wort at various stages of the brewing process.

aeration. The action of introducing air to the wort at various stages of the brewing process.

alcohol by volume (ABV). The percentage of volume of alcohol per volume of beer. To calculate the approximate volumetric alcohol content, subtract the final gravity from the original gravity and divide the result by 75. For example: $1.050 - 1.012 = 0.038 / 0.0075 = 5\%$ ABV.

alcohol by weight (ABW). The percentage weight of alcohol per volume of beer. For example: 3.2% alcohol by weight = 3.2 grams of alcohol per 100 centiliters of beer. Alcohol by weight can be converted to alcohol by volume by dividing by 0.795.

aldehyde. An organic compound that is a precursor to ethanol in a normal beer fermentation via the EMP pathway. In the presence of excess air, this reaction can be reversed, with alcohols being oxidized to very complex, unpleasant-tasting aldehydes, typically papery/cardboardy/sherry notes. These compounds are characterized as oxidized alcohols, with a terminal CHO group.

ale. 1. Historically, an unhopped malt beverage. 2. Now a generic term for hopped beers produced by top fermentation, as opposed to lagers, which are produced by bottom fermentation.

all-extract beer. A beer made with only malt extract as opposed to one made from malted barley, or a combination of malt extract and barley.

all-grain beer. A beer made with only malted barley as opposed to one made from malt extract, or from malt extract and malted barley.

alpha acid unit (AAU). The number of AAUs in a hop addition is equal to the weight of the addition in ounces times the alpha-acid percentage. Thus, 1 ounce of 5% alpha-acid hops contain 5 AAUs. AAU is the same as homebrewers bittering units.

alpha acid. One of the two soft resins in hops, it consists of a mixture of three closely related chemical compounds—humulone, co-humulone, and ad-humulone—and forms 2 to 14% of the total weight of hop cones and approximately 45% of their soft resins. Although the relative proportion of ad-humulone is fairly constant at 15%, the proportion of humulone and co-humulone varies from one hop variety to another. For example, the co-humulone content of Northern Brewer is close to 40%, whereas that of Fuggles is about 30%. Alpha acids have a low wort solubility, and about 90% of beer bitterness is caused by compounds that form during boiling, the most important of which are iso-alpha-acids (iso-humulones), which account for most of the bitterness. The conversion of alpha acids to iso-alpha-acids takes from one-half to one-and-a-half hours; however, this may vary because the solubility of alpha acids decreases with increasing wort gravity. In commercial brewing, iso-humulones are sometimes added in the form of isomerized extracts, usually after fermentation. During aging, alpha acids oxidize and lose approximately 30% of their bittering power after one year and about 40% after two years.

alpha amino nitrogen. See *amino acids.*

alpha amylase. A diastatic enzyme produced by malting barley, also known as a liquefying enzyme because it converts soluble malt starch into complex carbohydrates called dextrins during mashing. Alpha amylases work best at a pH of 5.6 to 5.8 and at a high temperature (150 °F/65.6 °C). They can withstand temperatures in excess of 163 °F (73 °C) but are destroyed at 176 °F (80 °C).

alt. A traditional style of beer brewed mainly in Düsseldorf but also in Münster, Korschenbroich, Krefeld, Issum, and a few other cities of North Rhineland–Westphalia. The German word *alt* means "old" or "ancient" and refers to the fact that these beers are brewed by the traditional method of top fermentation, predating the relatively new method of bottom fermentation introduced in the mid-eighteenth century and now predominant throughout Germany. Alt beers have a deep, luminous, copper color. They are brewed from dark malts, are well hopped, and display a slightly fruity, bittersweet flavor. Their alcohol content varies from 3.5 to 4% by weight (4.4 to 5% by volume) and are brewed from an original gravity of about 12.5

°Balling. Those from Düsseldorf have "Echte Düsseldorfer Altbier" written on the label.

ambient temperature. The surrounding temperature.

amino acids. Any of the organic acids whose molecules contain one or more acidic carboxyl groups (COOH), one or more amino groups (NH$_2$), and that polymerize to form peptides and proteins. Proteins are macromolecules composed of combinations of large numbers of the 20 different natural amino acids. During the beer-making process, amino acids are formed by the enzymatic degradation of such proteins. During kilning, amino acids combine with simple sugars to form colored compounds called melanoidins. The crucial issue associated with amino acids is their rate of uptake by yeast and the role they play in metabolism.

amylolytic enzyme. The enzyme that converts starch into soluble products such as sugars and dextrins.

amylose. Straight chain of native starch; a-D-glucose (glucose dehydrate) molecules joined by a-(1-4) links. Gives deep blue-black color with iodine.

anaerobic. Conditions under which there is not enough oxygen for respiratory metabolic function. Anaerobic microorganisms are those that can function without the presence of free molecular oxygen.

apparent attenuation. A simple measure of the extent of fermentation that a wort has undergone in the process of becoming beer. Using gravity units (GU), degrees Balling (°B), or degrees Plato (°P) units to express gravity, apparent attenuation is equal to the original gravity minus the terminal gravity divided by the original gravity. The result is expressed as a percentage and equals 65 to 80% for most beers.

apparent extract. A term used to indicate the apparent terminal gravity of a beer.

appellation. A name or designation.

astringency. A characteristic of beer taste mostly caused by tannins, oxidized tannins (phenols), and various aldehydes (in stale beer) that causes the mouth to pucker.

attenuate. Reduce the extract/density by yeast metabolism.

attenuation. The reduction in the wort's specific gravity caused by the transformation of sugars into alcohol and carbon-dioxide gas.

autolysis. The process of self-digestion of the body content of a cell by its own enzymes. The slow disintegration and breakdown of the membrane of yeast cells in the fermenting medium allow for the passage of nitrogen into the wort. If too pronounced the autolysis process gives a yeasty flavor to finished beer.

Balling. A saccharometer invented by Carl Joseph Napoleon Balling in 1843, it is a standard for the measurement of the density of solutions. It is calibrated for 63.5 °F (17.5 °C), and graduated in grams per hundred, giving a direct reading of the percentage of extract by weight per 100 grams solution. For example: 10 °Balling = 10 grams of sugar per 100 grams of wort.

Bavarian Purity Law of 1516. See *Reinheitsgebot.*

beta amylase. A diastatic enzyme produced by malting barley, also known as saccharifying enzyme because it converts dextrins and soluble starches into maltose, maltotriose, glucose, and alpha-limit dextrins. Beta amylase works best at a pH of 5 to 5.2 and at temperatures ranging from 135 to 150 °F (57 to 66 °C) and is destroyed at 176 °F (75 °C).

Biersteuergesetz. The beer tax law of Germany that governs not only the taxation of beer but the methods and processes of malting and brewing.

body. A qualitative indicator of the fullness or mouthfeel of a beer. Related to the proportion of unfermentable long-chain sugars or dextrins present in the beer. Also the consistency, thickness, and mouth-filling property of a beer. The sensation of palate fullness in the mouth ranges from full bodied to thin bodied.

bottle conditioned. Describes beer aged or carbonated in a bottle.

budding. The most common form of yeast cell reproduction. The cell increases in size, forming a rounded outgrowth that eventually separates into a daughter cell.

bung. 1. A sealing stopper, usually a cylindro-conical piece of wood, fitted into the mouth of the cask. A safety valve is sometimes used during secondary fermentation to maintain pressure at a maximum of 300 grams (g) per square centimeter (cm^2). 2. In homebrewing, the rubber or plastic seal into which the fermentation lock is fitted for secondary fermentation in carboys.

CaraHell. Similar to CaraPils.

CaraPils. Type of malt that is essentially a pale crystal malt and is used to add body and malty character to pale beers.

carbonates. Alkaline salts whose anions are derived from carbonic acid.

carbonate. The process of introducing carbon-dioxide gas into a liquid by: (1) injecting the finished beer with carbon dioxide; (2) adding young fermenting beer to finished beer for a renewed fermentation (kraeusening); (3) priming (adding sugar) to fermented wort prior to bottling, creating a secondary fermentation in the bottle; or (4) finishing fermentation under pressure.

carboy. A large glass, plastic, or earthenware bottle.

Glossary

cask. See *cask conditioned.*

cask conditioned. In Britain, ale conditioned in the cask is real ale. Casks of ale are delivered to the pubs, where they spend two to three days in cool cellars at a temperature of about 56 °F (13 °C) while conditioning is completed.

chill haze. Haziness caused by protein and tannin during the secondary fermentation.

chlorophenols. Strong and unpleasant-tasting chemical compounds formed by the combination of chlorine with a phenolic compound. Some are carcinogenic.

closed fermentation. Fermentation under closed, anaerobic conditions to minimize risk of contamination and oxidation.

coarse-grind/fine-grind extract difference. The difference in laboratory yield of malt samples, one of which is coarsely ground and one of which is finely ground. This measurement serves as an indicator of how mealy and/or how well modified a malt is.

cold trub. The precipitation of protein and tannin material to a fine coagulum during the cooling stage. It starts around 140 °F (60 °C) and increases as the temperature drops.

cold trub flotation. The process of removing cold trub from cooled wort by subjecting it to an excessive amount of air. Cold trub particles accumulate on the surface of the air bubbles as they rise from the bottom to the top of the flotation vessel, building a layer of foam at the surface of the wort. The wort is then drained from the bottom of the vessel, leaving behind the foam layer and, with it, the cold trub particles. The process may take place in pitched or unpitched wort.

conversion. The enzymatic transformation of starches into various fermentable and unfermentable sugars during the mashing process.

crop. The process of skimming or scooping yeast off the surface of top-fermenting ale during primary fermentation.

cylindro-conical tank. Fermentation or aging tank that has a cylindrically shaped body and a conically shaped bottom. Sometimes referred to as a uni-tank.

decoction mashing. One of the three mashing methods that is often used for bottom-fermenting beers. The process usually requires three vessels: a mash tun for mash mixing, a mash kettle (or copper or mash copper) for boiling, and a lauter tun (or clarifying tun) for straining. Mashing is carried out in a mash tun, and starts at a low temperature while portions of the mash are taken out and boiled in the mash kettle and later returned to the mash tun, thus gradually raising the temperature of the entire mash. The process can be repeated one or two times, taking five to six hours. The mash is then filtered in a separate vessel known as a lauter tun.

density. The measurement of the weight of a solution, as compared with the weight of an equal volume of pure water.

dextrin. Soluble polysaccharide fraction from hydrolysis of starch by heat, acid, or enzyme.

diacetyl. A volatile compound produced in beer by the oxidative decarboxylation of acetohydroxyl acids (2-acetalactate and 2-acetohydroxybutyrate) produced by yeasts. Diacetyl contributes a butterscotch flavor to beer.

diacetyl rest. A period of warm (60 to 72 °F/16 to 22 °C) maturation, usually 24 to 48 hours in length, which occurs at the end of the primary fermentation of a beer to accelerate the reduction of diacetyl into acetoin. Frequently used for the production of lager beers, the diacetyl rest is followed by aging.

diatomaceous earth. Also known as DE. The refined, fossilized skeletons of ancient marine organisms, called diatoms, which are frequently used as a filtration medium.

diet beer. Any beer low in sugar or carbohydrates but not necessarily low in calories. In Germany *diet bier* is designed for diabetics and has a relatively high alcoholic content of about 4.75% alcohol by weight or 6% alcohol by volume.

diketone. A class of aromatic, volatile compounds perceivable in minute concentrations, from yeast or *Pediococcus* bacteria metabolism. Most significantly the butter aroma of diacetyl, a vicinal diketone (VDK). The other significant compound relevant to brewing is 2,3-pentanedione.

dimethyl sulfide (DMS). An important sulfur-carrying compound originating in malt. Adds a crisp, "lagerlike" character at low levels, and corn or cabbage flavors at high levels.

disaccharides. Sugar group; two monosaccharide molecules joined by the removal of a water molecule.

doubling. Process of fermenting more than one batch of wort in an individual fermenter. Sometimes doubling may involve up to 12 batches of wort being pumped into one fermenter.

dry hopping. The addition of hops to the primary fermenter, the secondary fermenter, or to casked beer to add aroma and hop character to the finished beer without adding significant bitterness.

EBC **(European Brewery Convention).** Used as a measurement of color for beer or wort. See also *SRM*.

enzymes. Protein-based organic catalysts that affect changes in the compositions of the substances they act upon.

ester. A class of organic compounds created from the reaction of an alcohol and an organic acid. These tend to have fruity aromas and are detectable at low concentrations.

esters. Volatile flavor compounds that form through the interaction of organic acids with alcohols during fermentation and contribute to the fruity aroma and flavor of beer.

export. Also commonly known as Dortmunder. A blonde- or gold-colored, bottom-fermented beer from Dortmund (Westphalia), Germany's largest brewing city.

extract. The amount of dissolved materials in the wort after mashing and lautering malted barley and/or malt adjuncts such as corn and rice.

Fasching. A carnival or celebration, typically observed in the Catholic regions of Germany and Austria. Cologne is known as the Fasching capital of Germany.

fatty acids. A group of saturated monobasic aliphatic carboxylic acids, all of which impart a rancid soapy flavor to beer, contribute to its staling, and affect its head retention.

final specific gravity. The specific gravity of a beer when fermentation is complete.

fining. A clarifying process that adds organic or mineral settling agents during secondary fermentation to precipitate colloidal matter through coagulation or adsorption.

first runnings. The first batch of wort to be filtered in the straining vat. It is richer in extract than following batches.

flocculation. The phenomenon by which yeast cells aggregate into masses toward the end of the fermentation process and sink to the bottom, thus contributing to the clarification of the beer. The ability of a yeast (either top- or bottom-fermenting) to flocculate or settle varies with the strain of yeast.

Fraternity of Saint Peter of Milano. Original brewers' organization or association of Cologne, officially formed in 1396.

friability. Term and measure of how mealy and/or how well modified a malt is.

fusel alcohols. See *higher alcohols.*

Gambrinus. A corruption or contraction of the name Jan Primus, Duke Jean I of Brabant, Louvain, and Antwerp, born 1251 in Bourguignon and killed 1295 in a duel or in a tournament in Bar. He is the second patron (not a saint) of brewers and the first patron of beer lovers. He was not a brewer but a popular ruler well liked by the brewers' association of Brussels. Gambrinus was instrumental in helping the residents of Cologne and the Dukes of Looz and Juelich win the battle of Worringen in 1288. This victory was critical in cementing the political position of Cologne's guilds at the time.

germination. The second stage of the beermaking process that drains the steeped barley grains and allows them to sprout for seven to nine days. The process may be accelerated by the use of such products as gibberellic acid or may be prolonged up to 11 or

13 days for a more thorough disintegration of the malt. While germinating, the embryo produces the enzyme amylase (sometimes called diastase), which will later convert some of the starch of the endosperm into the maltose and dextrins. This treatment of the barley grains follows cleaning, sorting, grading, and steeping and takes place at 50 to 68 °F (10 to 20 °C).

grainy. Tastes like cereal or raw grain.

green beer. Newly fermented beer before maturing or lagering.

green malt. Malt that has been steeped and germinated and is ready for kilning.

gruit. A mixture of herbs and spices—principally sweet gale (bog-myrtle), marsh (wild rosemary), coriander, yarrow, and milfoil, as well as other ingredients such as juniper berries, caraway seed, aniseed, ginger, nutmeg, and cinnamon—once used to flavor English and European ales before the introduction of hops.

guild. A medieval association of merchants or craftsmen.

helles. Style of pale lager that is commonly brewed in Bavaria.

higher alcohols. Alcohols that have a higher boiling point than ethanol and are derived from keto acids during the yeast protein synthesis. The formation of higher alcohols varies with yeast strain and yeast growth, fermentation temperature (an increase in temperature promotes the formation of alcohols), and fermentation (in some cases a stirred fermentation produces more alcohols). There are two classes of higher (fusel) alcohols: (1) volatile alcohols, most often called aliphatic alcohols (i.e., propyl alcohols, butyl alcohol, amyl alcohols); and (2) nonvolatile alcohols (i.e., phenol alcohols like tyrosal).

higher aliphatic alcohols. See *higher alcohols.*

homebrewers bittering units (HBU). A formula adopted by the American Homebrewers Association to measure bitterness of beer. Example: 1.5 ounces of hops at 10% alpha acid for 5 gallons: 1.5 × 10 = 15 HBU per 5 gallons. Same as AAU.

hop-bitter lager beer. Style of top-fermenting beer that directly preceded Kölsch in the evolution of Cologne's beers. Also referred to as alt and wiess. This style had a starting gravity of 8 to 9 °Plato, was golden in color, and was very highly hopped.

hop extract. Bitter resins and hop oils that are extracted from hops by organic solvents, usually methylene chloride, carbon dioxide, or hexane, rather than by hot water, as are tannins, sugars, and proteins. The solvents and water are later removed by evaporation. The use of such extracts is increasing in the brewing industry because they store well, are less bulky, require no refrigeration and a shorter boiling time, and do not require straining of spent hops. Hop extracts are sometimes isomerized by alkalis or by magnesium slats at neutrality, or by exposure to light of a specific wavelength.

Iso-alpha-acid hop extract (or isomerized hop extract) is added as late as possible, usually during secondary fermentation.

hop pellets. Highly processed hops consisting of finely powdered hop cones compressed into pea-sized tablets that are used in both home and commercial brewing. Regular hop pellets are, by weight, 20 to 30% stronger than the same variety in loose form; 1 pound of hop cones yields about 10 to 12 ounces of pellets. Concentrated pellets, as used in the brewing industry, are first processed to remove the nonresinous material, thus reducing the weight and volume. Standardized pellets are made from blends of hops to obtain a specific alpha acid level. Hop pellets keep better when stored cold in a sealed container.

hot trub. The coagulation and precipitation of protein and polyphenol matter during the boiling stage. In homebrewing, hot-break trub can be improved by the addition of Irish moss during the last 15 minutes of the boil or it can be removed with a hop-back filtration of the wort or by allowing the hot wort to settle out before drawing it to the wort chiller.

infusion mashing. One of the three mashing methods and the traditional method for top-fermenting beer. The process is carried out at a constant temperature and in a single vessel, which is a mash tun fitted with a perforated false bottom. The mash, which is not boiled, is sprayed with hot water to raise the mashing temperature gradually at 149 to 154 °F (65 to 68 °C) for one to two hours. After mashing is complete, the wort is drawn through the slotted base, which can be opened to filter the liquid while straining the spent grains.

international bitterness unit (IBU or BU). This is a standard unit that measures the concentration of iso-alpha acids in milligrams per liter (parts per million). Most procedures will also measure a small amount of uncharacterized soft resins, so IBUs are generally 5 to 15% higher than iso-alpha acid concentrations.

inverted sugar. Processed common sugar (sucrose) separated into two sugars, fructose and glucose, by a modification of the molecular structure. It is obtained industrially by the inversion of sucrose with diluted acid, usually sulfuric acid, into equal parts of glucose and fructose. It does not contain dextrins and can be used as an adjunct or for priming.

iodine test. A simple test to ascertain if all the malt starch has been converted to maltose. It consists of adding a drop of tincture of iodine to a drop of cold wort on a clean white saucer. If the color remains iodine-brown, the starch conversion is complete, whereas a blue or purplish blue coloration is indicative of the presence of starch and that mashing must continue. Since iodine is toxic, the test sample must not be returned to the mash.

isinglass. A gelatinous substance made from the swim bladder of certain fish and added to beer as a fining agent.

isothermic. A change or process that takes place at one temperature.

keutebier. Northern German style of beer made with malt and hops that became popular in Cologne during the fifteenth century and catalyzed the evolution of beer from gruit to beer as we know it today.

kilning. The final stage in the malting of barley that prepares it for use by the brewer. Kilning reduces the moisture contained in the grain to approximately 4% and also roasts the malt to some extent. The degree of roasting affects the flavor and color of the malt as well as of the beer it produces.

Kölsch. 1. (n) A pale, golden ale that is brewed in Cologne, Germany, and its outlying towns. It is protected by an appellation under German law, meaning it cannot be called Kölsch unless its geographic origin is specified. 2. (adj.) Word used to describe something that is of Cologne.

Kölsch Konvention. Pact signed in 1986 by 24 breweries in and around Cologne that is recognized by the German government and gives these breweries the exclusive right to use the word *Kölsch* to describe their beer. See *Kölsch*.

kraeusen. 1. (n.) The rocky head of foam that appears on the surface of the wort during fermentation. Also used to describe the period of fermentation characterized by a rich foam head. 2. (v.) To add fermenting wort to fermented beer to induce carbonation through a secondary fermentation.

Lactobacillus. Species of bacteria that ferments wort sugars to produce lactic acid. Although considered undesirable in most breweries and beer styles, it plays a significant role in the production of some beers, such as Berliner weiss and lambics.

lager. 1. (n.) A generic term for any bottom-fermented beer. Lager brewing is now the predominant brewing method worldwide except in Britain, where top-fermented ales dominate. 2. (v.) To store beer at near-zero temperatures in order to precipitate yeast cells and proteins and improve taste.

lag phase. Associated with yeast viability, the time between yeast pitching and the start of activity as signaled by the appearance of foam at the surface of the wort. During this time, the yeast cells use oxygen for sterol synthesis and become larger but do not produce any buds.

lag time. See *lag phase.*

last runnings. The last of the wort to be filtered from the straining vat.

lauter. The process of separating the clear liquid from the mash and husks.

lauter tun. A vessel in which the mash settles and the grains are removed from the sweet wort through a straining process. It has a false slotted bottom and spigot.

malt. Barley that has been steeped in water, germinated, then dried in kilns. This process develops enzymes that convert protein and starch to amino acids and sugars during the mashing process.

malt extract. A thick syrup or dry powder prepared from malt.

maltose. A disaccharide composed of two glucose molecules, and the primary sugar obtained by diastatic hydrolysis of starch. It has one-third the sweetness of sucrose.

maltose rest. See *beta amylase.*

mashing. Mixing ground malt with water to extract the fermentables, degrade haze-forming proteins, and convert grain starches to fermentable sugars and nonfermentable carbohydrates.

mead. An alcoholic beverage produced by fermenting honey and water. Mead can be dry, sweet, or sparkling.

melanoidins. Color-producing compounds produced through a long series of chemical reactions that begin with the combination of a sugar and an amino acid.

modification. 1. The physical and chemical changes that occur in barley during malting, in which complex molecules are broken down to simpler, soluble molecules. 2. The degree to which malt has undergone these changes, as determined by the growth of the acrospire.

mouthfeel. See *body*.

open fermenter. Traditional fermentation vessel that is shallow relative to its height and is open to the atmosphere.

original gravity. The specific gravity of wort previous to fermentation. A measure of the total amount of dissolved solids in wort.

oxidation. 1. The combining of oxygen with other molecules, often causing off-flavors, as with oxidized alcohols to form aldehydes. 2. A reaction in which the atoms in an element lose electrons and its valence is correspondingly increased (oxidation-reduction reaction).

parti-gyle. An arcane system of brewing in which the first runnings of wort are taken to make a high-gravity beer, and the grain is then remashed to create another brew. This can be done yet again to make a third brew, all from the same grains. There is usually no sparging involved when using the parti-gyle system. With the advent of more sophisticated equipment that allowed lautering and sparging, the parti-gyle system of brewing lost favor around the end of the nineteenth century.

pH. A measure of acidity or alkalinity of a solution, usually on a scale of 1 to 14, where 7 is neutral, 1 is most acidic, and 14 is most basic.

phenolic. Describes an unpleasant solvent-, medicinal-, or chemical-like flavor.

phosphate. A salt or ester of phosphoric acid.

pitching. Inoculating sterile wort with a vigorous yeast culture.

Plato, degrees. Commercial brewers' standard for the measurement of the density of solutions, expressed as the equivalent weight of cane sugar in solution (calibrated on grams of sucrose per 100 grams of solution). Like degrees Balling, but degrees Plato computations are more exact.

Plato saccharometer. A saccharometer that expresses specific gravity as extract weight in a 100-gram solution at 68 °F (20 °C). A revised, more accurate version of Balling, developed by Dr. Plato.

polymer. A compound molecule formed by the joining of many smaller identical units. For example, polyphenols from phenols, polypeptides from peptides.

polyphenol. Complexes of phenolic compounds involved in chill haze formation and oxidative staling.

ppm. Parts per million. Equal to milligrams per liter (mg/l). The measurement of particles of matter in solution.

precipitation. A clarification process that coagulates impurities, causing them to come out of solution.

precursor. The starting materials or inputs for a chemical reaction.

primary fermentation. The first stage of fermentation, during which most fermentable sugars are converted to ethyl alcohol and carbon dioxide.

priming. The act of adding priming sugar to a still (or flat) beer so that it may develop carbonation.

priming solution. A solution of sugar in water added to aged beer at bottling to induce a second fermentation (bottle conditioning).

priming sugar. Corn or cane sugar added in small amounts to bulk beer prior to racking or to each bottle prior to capping to induce a new fermentation in the bottle and thus create carbonation. Home-brewers use about three-quarters to one cup of sugar per five-gallon batch of beer.

protein. Generally amorphous and colloidal complex amino acid containing about 16% nitrogen with carbon, hydrogen, oxygen, and possibly sulfur, phosphorous, and iron. True protein has a molecular weight of 17,000 to 150,000; in beer, protein will have been largely decomposed to a molecular weight of 5,000 to 12,000 (albumin or proteoses), 400 to 1,500 (peptides), or amino acids. Protein as a haze fraction ranges from molecular weight 10,000 to 100,000 (average 30,000), and as the stabilizing component of foam, from 12,000 to 20,000.

proteolysis. The hydrolysis of a protein molecule into amino acids by proteolytic enzymes.

proteolytic enzyme. An enzyme that hydrolyzes complex proteins into simpler soluble bodies.

racking. The process of transferring beer from one container to another, especially into the final package (bottles, kegs, etc.).

Reinheitsgebot. A German law of which the title signifies "pledge of purity" or "order of purity." This purity law governs the production and quality of beer in Germany. Inspired by an earlier law instituted by Duke Albert IV in 1487, William VI, the elector of Bavaria, decreed in 1516 that only water, malted barley, malted wheat, and hops could be used to make beer. Yeast was not included but taken for granted. This law was ruled to be protective in 1987 and was repealed, allowing beers with adjuncts to be brewed and sold in Germany. However, all German brewers signed a collective agreement to continue to adhere to the Reinheitsgebot.

residual alkalinity. In the mashing process, carbonates and bicarbonates decrease mash acidity, and alkali- and alkaline earth metals increase mash acidity (in brewing the metals involved are essentially potassium, calcium, and magnesium). In the case of brewing water, the alkalinity (or acidity decreasing) of the carbonates and bicarbonates is offset by the acidity of calcium and magnesium in stoichiometric proportions. In water sources, the acidity increasing effect of calcium and magnesium almost never equalizes the alkaline effect of the carbonates and bicarbonates, thus, the alkalinity (or carbonate hardness) that is not offset by calcium and magnesium is the residual alkalinity.

resin. The gummy organic substance produced by certain plants and trees. Humulone and lupulone, for example, are bitter resins produced by the hop flower.

rest. Mash rest. Holding the mash at a specific temperature to induce certain enzymatic changes.

runnings. The wort or sweet liquid that is collected during the lautering of the wet mash.

saccharification. The naturally occurring process in which malt starch is converted into fermentable sugars, primarily maltose. Also called mashing because saccharification occurs during the mash rest.

saccharification rest. A stage of the mashing process during which complex glucose chains are broken down into fermentable sugars. Saccharification is accomplished by alpha amylase and beta amylase acting in concert to reduce complex glucose chains. Alpha amylase is most active at temperatures between 131 and 158 °F (55 and 70 °C). Beta amylase is most active at temperatures between 113 and 149 °F (45 and 65 °C). This stage of mashing requires a temperature range between 145 and 158 °F (63 and 70 °C). Higher mash temperatures produce more full-bodied worts because beta amylase becomes deactivated sooner at higher temperatures. Lower mash temperatures yield more fermentable sugars. Rest durations vary with temperatures. Lower mash temperatures yield more fermentable sugars. Rest duration varies with temperature. At higher temperatures, a 20- to 40-minute rest will accomplish conversion. At lower temperatures, a rest of 45 minutes to two hours is required.

saccharometer. An instrument that determines the sugar concentration of a solution by measuring the specific gravity.

Saccharomyces cerevisae. Scientific name for top-fermenting yeast.

Saccharomyces uvarum. Scientific name for bottom-fermenting yeast. Also known as *Saccharomyces carlsbergensis.*

schankbier. Term used to describe one of the starting gravity categories in Germany. Schankbier must have a starting gravity between 7 and 8 °Plato.

secondary fermentation. 1. The second, slower stage of fermentation, which, depending on the type of beer, lasts from a few weeks to many months. 2. A fermentation occurring in bottles or casks and initiated by priming or by adding yeast.

sheet filter. A plate and frame filter that uses single-direction, reusable cellulose sheets.

silica gel. A hard, amorphous, granular form of hydrated silica that absorbs nitrogen matter in beer.

sparge. The even distribution or spray of hot water over the saccharified mash to rinse free the extract from the grist.

sparging. Spraying the mash with hot water to leach the remaining malt sugar. This is done at the end of the mashing (saccharification) process.

specific gravity. A measure of the density of a liquid or solid as compared to that of water, which is given the value 1.000 at 39.2 °F (4 °C). For the sake of accuracy, the specific gravity of liquids should always be measured as closely as possible to that temperature. The specific gravity is a dimensionless quantity (with no accompanying units) because it is expressed as a ratio in which all units of measurement cancel. Abbrev.: SG, s.g.

SRM (Standard Reference Method) and EBC (European Brewery Convention). Two different analytical methods of describing color, developed by comparing color samples. Degrees SRM, approximately equivalent to degrees Lovibond, are used by the ASBC (American Society of Brewing Chemists), while degrees EBC are European units. The following equations show approximate conversions: (EBC) = 2.65 × (SRM) − 1.2; SRM = 0.377 × (EBC) + 0.46.

stammtisch. Large table commonly found in German pubs, reserved for the regulars or special guests of the proprietor.

starch. Any group of carbohydrates or polysaccharides secreted in the form of granules by certain cereals, composed of about one-quarter amylose (inner shell) and three-quarters amylopectin (outer shell). Starch hydrolyzes to yield dextrins and maltose through the action of amylases. Barley starch is enclosed in the endosperm and constitutes 63 to 65% of the weight of two-row barley and 58% of the weight of six-row barley.

starter. A separate batch of fermenting beer added to the bitter wort once it has cooled down to 70 °F (21 °C). In homebrewing, it is prepared by pitching yeast in a quart of wort cooled to about 75 °F (24 °C), preferably one or two days in advance.

steeping. The initial processing step in malting, where the raw barley is soaked in water and periodically aerated to induce germination.

strike temperature. The water temperature at mashing-in; generally somewhat higher than the target mash temperature to compensate for heat uptake by the grist.

tannin. Any of a group of organic compounds contained in certain cereal grains and other plants. Hop tannins have the ability to help in the precipitation of haze-forming protein materials during the boiling (hot break) and cooling (cold break) of the wort. Tannins are mainly present in the bracts and strigs of the hop cone and imparts an astringent taste to beer. Also call "hop tannin" to distinguish it from tannins originating from malted barley. The greater part of the tannin content of the wort is derived from malt husks, but malt tannins differ chemically from hop tannins. Non-technical term used for phenols.

terminal extract. The density of fully fermented beer.

trub. Flocks of haze-forming particles resulting from the precipitation of proteins, hop oils, and tannins during the boiling and cooling stages of brewing.

uni-tank. Brewing vessel used as both a fermenting and a conditioning tank.

viscosity. The resistance of a fluid to flow.

volatile. Readily vaporized, referring especially to esters, essential oils, and higher alcohols.

vollbier. "Full beer" is the most common starting gravity category in Germany. Vollbier must have a starting gravity between 11 and 14 °Plato.

vorlauf. German term for recirculation of wort through the grain bed.

water hardness. The degree of hardness of water caused by the presence of mineral elements dissolved into it. It is expressed, in metric units, in parts of calcium carbonate per million parts of water; in England, in Clark degrees, water hardness is valued as 1 part of calcium carbonate per 70,000 parts of water; in France, a degree of hardness is 1 milligram (mg) of calcium carbonate per 1,000 liters (l) of water; in Germany it is valued as 1 mg of calcium oxide per 1,000 l of water. The German figure, when multiplied by 17.9, gives parts per million of calcium carbonate.

Weihenstephan. The oldest brewery in the world. Now a brewery and brewing school located just outside of Munich.

weissbier. "White beer" is the generic term used for German-style wheat beers.

whirlpool. An apparatus for the clarification of beer, consisting of a large, cylindrical tank about as tall as it is broad. The wort is introduced at high speed through a pipe set tangentially at about midpoint in the vertical wall. As wort comes to rest in the tank, the trub, or hot break, deposits as a cone at the bottom by a process of sedimentation.

wiess. A more traditional version of Kölsch that is unfiltered.

wort. Mash extract (sweet wort); the hopped sugar solution before pitching, before it is fermented into beer.

yield difference. Difference in yield of extract in the laboratory and in a brewery for a given malt. Extract values are determined in a laboratory and are regarded as the greatest possible yield because the sample grist is very fine, and the rest at saccharification temperatures is long. Brewery grist is coarser and sacchrification rests are shorter, so the extract yield of a malt in a brewery is less than it is in the lab. Modern breweries are able to realize a yield difference that is within 1% of the lab value. For example, if the lab extract value is 80% dry weight, the brewery should have a yield that is 79% or slightly higher.

yield of extract. The percentage of extractable dry matter in the grist; that is, the total amount of dry matter that passes into solution in the wort during mashing.

Bibliography

Dornbusch, Horst D. *Prost! The Story of German Beer.* Boulder, Colo.: Brewers Publications, 1997.

Sion-Stiftung, Hans. *Kölner Brauhaus Wanderweg.* Cologne: Druckerei J. P. Bachem GmbH & Co. KG, 1995.

Hoffman, M. *5000 Jahre Bier.* Nürnberg, Germany: Verlag Hans Carl, 1956.

Jackson, Michael. *The New World Guide to Beer.* Philadelphia: Running Press Book Publishers, 1993.

Malone, Pat. "Kölsch Beer." *All About Beer* (October 1987).

Mathar, Franz, and Rudolf Spiegel. *Kölsche Bier- und Brauhäuser.* Cologne: Greven Verlag, 1989.

Narziss, Ludwig. *Abriß der Bierbrauerei.* Stuttgart, Germany: Ferdinand Enke Verlag, 1986.

Papazian, Charlie. *Home Brewer's Gold.* New York: Avon Books, 1997.

Rabin, Dan, and Carl Forget. *The Dictionary of Beer and Brewing.* 2d ed. Boulder, Colo.: Brewers Publications, 1998.

Rick, Detlef. *Private Manuscript about Kölsch.* Forthcoming.

Schönfeld, Franz. *Obergärige Biere und ihre Herstellung.* Berlin: Verlag von Paul Parey, 1938.

Sinz, Herbert. *1000 Jahre Kölsch Bier, eine Chronik für Genießer.* Pulheim, Germany: Rhein, Eifel, Mosel-Verlag, 1985.

Warner, Eric. *German Wheat Beer.* Classic Beer Style Series. Boulder, Colo.: Brewers Publications, 1992.

Index

Please note that page references in italic indicate photographs.

Acetaldehyde concentrations, 61

Acetoin, 61

Adler Brauerei, 137, 139

Adler- und Hirsch Brauerei, 137

Aeration, 91

Aging
  and fermentation, 91-99, *94,*
    97, 115-16
  tanks, 96-97, *98*

Alcohol by volume (ABV), 48-
    50, 72

Alcohol by weight (ABW), 50

Alcohol content, 48-50, 72

Alcohol-free beers, 50, 53, 141,
    148, 149

Alcohol-free Kölsch, 148, 149

All-extract beers, 120-21

All-grain beers, 121-27

Alpha-acid content of hops, 84,
    118-19

Alpha amino acids, 65-66, 76

Alt *(altrheinisches-hopfenbitteres*
    lagerbier), 32-33

Altstadt-Bräu Joh. Sion KG,
    129-30

American
  hops, 70
  lager, 48

American Homebrewers
    Association, 127

American-Style Kölsch, recipe,
    123-25

American Tettnang hops, 70

Amino acids, 65-66, 76

Aroma hops, 52, 69, 70, 85

Aroma profile, 59-61

Association of Cologne
    Breweries, 40

Attenuation, 46, 48-49, 91

Barley, 7, 20, 64, 68

Battle of Worringen (1288), 16,
    17-18

Bavarian Brewers Association, 17

Bavarian *helles,* 48, 50, 100

Bavarian Purity Law (1516), 20, 47

Index

Becker, Heinrich, 134

Beer Drive tanks, 101

Beichtstuhl (confessional), 110, 112, *112*

Bergische Löwen Brauerei GmbH & Co. KG, 130

Bielsteiner Brauerei, 139

Biersteuergesetz, 46-47, 54, 66, 85, 99, 102

Bittering hops, 51-52, 69, 85

Bitter units (BU), 51-52

Black market "hacker" brewers, 23

Bock beers, 47, 141

Bonn-Bonn Kölsch, recipe, 127-28

Bottle conditioning, 116-17

Bottled Kölsch, 53

Bottling, 28, 99, *100,* 101, 102

Bottom-fermented lager, 35-36

Bottom-fermenting yeast (*Saccharomyces uvarum*), 60

Bottom harvesting, yeast, 74-75, 97

Brau & Brunnen, 43, 130, 154

Brauerei Peter Schopen GmbH, 130-31

Brauerei zur Malzmühle Schwartz KG, 131-33, *132*

Brauhaus zur Garde AG, 133-34, 155

Breweries. *See specific breweries*

Brewers

    black market "hacker," 23

    homebrewers, 4-5, 10

    life of, 22

    See also Hobby brewers, tips for; Guilds; Recipes for Kölsch; *specific breweries*

Brewers Guild of Brussels, 17

Brewers Guild of Cologne, 10

Brewing

    commercial, 5-6, 9-16

    at elevation, 83

    lager brewing, 22-23, 26

    monastic brewing, 6-7, 10-11, 13

    tradition of, 4-6

    See also Fermentation, maturation, packaging

Brewing Kölsch

    alpha acid content of hops, 64, 84, 118-19

    amino acids, 65-66, 76

    aroma hops, adding, 85

    bittering hops, adding, 85

    bottom harvesting yeast, 74-75, 97

calcium chloride (CaCl$_2$),
72-73
cold sedimentation, 86
cold trub flotation, 86-87
cold trub separation, 85-86
and coloring agents, 66
decoction mashing, 51, 75,
76, 78, 81-83
at elevation, 83
European pale malts, 68
finishing hops, adding, 85
and foam, 76-77
free amino nitrogen, 71
German Pilsner malt, 64-65
German Wheat Malt, 67-68
gypsum (CaSO$_4$), 72-73
hops, German, 46, 63, 68-70,
69, 85
ingredients for, 63-64
lag time, 71
lautering, 77, 78, 83
liquor to grist ratio, 79
maltose rest, 79-80
malts and grain bill, 63, *64,*
64-68, *66*
mashing techniques, 75-83
mash pH, 71, 72
multitemperature infusion
mash program, 79-80

North American pale malts, 68
oxidation, 77, 78
precipitation, 71
protein rest, 82
proteins, 65
residual alkalinity, 70-73
saccharification rest, 80
Saccharomyces cerevisiae
(top-fermenting yeast),
60, 73-74
single-infusion mashing, 75,
78, 80-81
sparging, 79, 83
step mash program, 76, 77-83
sweeteners, use of, 66
tannins, 71
top-cropping yeast, 74-75, 97
water, Kölsch, 63, 70-73
whirlpool rest, 85
wort boiling and hopping,
83-87, *84, 86*
yeast, 63, 73-75
See also Fermentation, maturation, packaging; Recipes
for Kölsch
Brühler Brauerei-Gesellschaften
GmbH, 142
Brühler Leicht, 143
BU (bitter units), 51-52

Budding, 93

Bunging, 97, 98

Bürger Kölsch, 134, 155

Calcium chloride (CaCl$_2$), 72-73

Cans, 101, 101-2

CaraHell malt, 64

CaraPils malt, 50, 64

Carbonation

    levels of, 53-54

    natural, 98-99, 116-17

    and packaging, 115-17

"Cask" Kölsch, 117

Charlemagne (Karl the Great),

    5-6

Chemical composition. See

    Sensory profile, chemical

    composition

Christianity, impact of

    on pubs, 110, 112

    on taxation, 18

    in thirteenth-century, 11, 13

Clarification, 99-100

"Clean" ale, 60

Coasters and beer consumption,

    109-10

Cold

    aging, 98

    sedimentation, 86

trub flotation, 86-87

trub separation, 85-86

Colner Brauer Corporation

    (Corporation of Cologne

    Brewers), 25

    See also Fraternity of Saint

    Peter of Milano

Cölner Hofbräu P. Josef Früh,

    Köln, 134-36, 135

Cologne and Kölsch beer

    alt (altrheinisches-hopfenbit-

    teres lagerbier), 32-33

    Battle of Worringen, 16, 17-18

    black market "hacker" brew-

    ers, 23

    bottling, impact of, 28

    bottom-fermented lager, 35-36

    brewers, life of, 22

    brewing tradition, 4-6

    and Christianity, 11, 13, 18,

    110, 112

    commercial brewing, 5-6,

    9-16

    distilling, 24

    echt Kölsch (filtered), 35

    Fasching event, 23-24

    first brews of, 3-4

    Fraternity of Saint Peter of

    Milano, 10-11, 15-16, 25

and French occupation, 25-26

gruit beers, 3, 7, 8-9, 20, 21

Guild Alliance of Cologne, *12,* 13

guilds, 9-16, *12,* 21-22, 24-34

herbs, use of, 8

homebrewers, 4-5, 10

hoppebier, 4

hops, first use of, 3, 7, 19-20

and indirect heated kiln, 2, 29, 32-33

and Industrial Revolution, 29

keutebier beers, 3, 19, 20, 25

Kölsch Konvention, 2-3, 9, 39-42, *41,* 104

Kölsch wiess, 32-33, 35, 100

"kraut" beer, birth of, 6-9

and lager brewing, 22-23, 26

large breweries, growth of, 26

malt production, 24

mead beers, 3, 7

during the Middle Ages, 16-25

monastic brewing, 6-7, 10-11, 13

pale beers, 1-2, 25-34

and political issues, 18-19

Primus, Jan (Gambrinus), 16-17, *17*

pubs, nineteenth-century, 30-31

purity laws, 20-21

and taxation, 18-21, 23, 36

thousand-bomb attack on, 37-38

in today's market, 42-44

top-fermenting style of beer, 4

and unions, 28, *28*

and World War I and II, 34-39

See also Cologne's classic cuisine; Drinking Kölsch; *specific breweries*

Cologne Brewers Association, 42

Cologne Brewers Corporation, 40

Cologne's classic cuisine

foderkaat (menu), 157

halver hahn (half rooster), 157

Himmel un Aed (Heaven and Earth), 161-62

Klatschkies Met Oellich, 158-59

Kölsch caviar, 158

Muuzemandeln, 162-63

Rievkooche, 159-60

Soorbrode (*sauerbraten*), 160-61

specialities, disappeared, 158

Color, straw-gold, 45, 50-51

Coloring agents, use of, 66

Commercial brewing, 5-6, 9-16

Confessional (beichtstuhl), 110, 112, *112*

Cooling of beer, 95-96

Cropping, yeast, 90, 94

DAB (Dortmunder Aktienbrauerei), 134, 155

Decoction mashing
basics of, 81-83
for darker beers, 51, 68, 76
and foam thickness, 76
single decoction mash, 75

Diacetyl
levels, 60-61, 63, 65, 72, 94
rests, 95

Diatomaceous earth, use of, 99

Dimethyl sulfide (DMS), 61, 83

Distilling, 24

Dom-Brauerei GmbH, 136-38, 153

Dom brewery, 37

Dominicans, 11

Dom Kölsch, 138

Dom Pils, 138

Doppelbock, 46

Dormagener Brewery, 133-34

Dormagener Kölsch, 134

Dortmunder Aktienbrauerei (DAB), 134, 155

Dortmunder Hansa Brauerei, 154

Dortmunder Union-Brauerei, 144

Doubling, 94-95, 96

Draft Kölsch, 53-54

Drinking Kölsch
and *beichtstuhl* (confessional), 110, 112, *112*
coasters and consumption, 109-10
Köbes (waiters), 105, 107-9, *108*
and Kölsch Konvention, 104
in a Pinten (mug), 105-6
and porcelain saucers, 110, *111*
and the publican, 112
in a Schnelle, 106, *106*
in a Stange, 103-6, *104*
"stood in the chalk," 110
"written up," 110

Dry hopping, 52

EBC (European Brewery Convention), 45, 51

Echt Kölsch (filtered), 35
Einfachbier, 50, 66
Elevation and brewing, 83
End-attenuated, 95
Erzquell-Brauerei Bielstein Haas
    & Co. KG, 139
Essener Aktien-Brauerei, 137
Ester, 63, 94
Ethyl-acetate concentrations,
    59-50
European Brewery Convention
    (EBC), 45, 51
European pale malts, 68

Fasching event, 23-24
Fermentarii, 8
Fermentation, maturation,
    packaging
  aeration, 91
  and aging, 91-99, *94, 97,*
    115-16
  aging tanks, 96-97, 98
  attenuation, 46, 48-49, 91
  Beer Drive tanks, 101
  bottling, 99, *100,* 101, 102
  bottom harvesting yeast, 74-
    75, 97
  budding, 93

bunging process, *97,* 98
by-products of fermentation,
    54-61, 71-72
cans, *101,* 101-2
carbonation, 98-99
clarification, 99-100
cold aging, 98
cooling of beer, 95-96
cropping, yeast, 90, 94
diacetyl rests, 95
diatomaceous earth, use of, 99
doubling, 94-95, 96
end-attenuated, 95
finings, use of, 99, 100
gelatin, use of, 100
green-beer, 96, 97-98
in ninth century, 8
packaging, *101,* 101-2
pressure fermentation, 93-94
repitching yeast, 90
sheet filters, use of, 99
silica gels, use of, 99
stabilizing agents, 99-100
temperatures for fermentation,
    91-92, 113-14
tips for, 113-15
top-cropping yeast, 74-75, 97
vessels for fermentation, 92-93

Fermentation, maturation,
   packaging (*continued*)
   wood chips, use of, 99
   yeast pitching, 89-91
   yeasts, nonflocculating, 96, 99
Filtering, 46, 72, 99-100, 116
Finings, for clarification, 99, 100
Finishing hops, 70, 85
Fix, George (recipe by), 127-28
Flavor profile, 50-59
Foam, 76-77
Fraternities, 9-16, *12,* 21-22,
   24-34
Fraternity of Saint Peter of
   Milano, 10-11, 15-16, 25
Free amino nitrogen, 71
French occupation, free-trade,
   25-26
Früh, Peter Josef, 134-35
Früh am Dom, 136
Früh am Hof brewery, 38
Früh im Veedel, 136
Früh Kölsch, 135-36

GABF (Great American Beer
   Festival), 117-18
Gaffel-Kölsch Classic, 148, 149
Gambrinus (Primus, Jan), 16-
   17, *17*

Ganser, Peter, 140
Ganserator, 141
Ganser Brauerei GmbH & Co.
   KG, 140-41
Ganser Kölsch, 140-41
Ganser Kölsch Light, 141
Ganser Kölsch Zero, 141
"Gap" beers, 47
Garde Kölsch, 134
Gebrüder Sünner GmbH & Co.
   KG, 141-42
Gelatin, for clarification, 100
German Brewers Association, 27
German Brewery Holding, 130,
   144, 145
German Brewery Museum
   (Munich), 17
German Pilsner, 33, 42, 48,
   50, 100
German Pilsner malt, 64-65
German Wheat Beer (Warner), 55
German wheat malt, 67-68
Germany Brewery Holding, 43
Gerresheim monastery, 6-7
Giesler, Friedrich, 142
Giesler Alt, 143
Giesler Brauerei GmbH & Co.,
   142-43
Giesler Kölsch, 142-43

Giesler Pilsner, 143

Gilden Kölsch, 130

Gilden Kölsch Brauerei, 144

Great American Beer Festival
(GABF), 117-18

Green beer *(jungbier)*, 31, 96,
97-98

Gruit beers, 3, 7, 8-9, 20, 21

Guild Alliance of Cologne, *12*, 13

Guilds, 9-16, *12*, 21-22, 24-34

Gypsum (CaSO$_4$), 72-73

Half rooster *(halver hahn)*, 157

Hallertau hops, 52, 69, 85

Halv und halv, 31

HBU (homebrew bittering unit),
119

Helles beers, 48, 50, 100

Herbs, use of, 8

Hermann of Hessia,
Archbishop, 9

Hersbrucker hops, 52, 69, 85

Heumarkt, 132

Higher alcohols, 58-59

Himmel un Aed (Heaven and
Earth), recipe, 161-62

Hirsch Beer, 137

Hirsch Brauerei Goeter &
Steingröver, 136-37

Hirsch Edel Pils, 137

Hirsch Gold Export, 137

Hitdorfer Brauerei, 138

Hobby brewers, tips for
aging, 115-16

alpha acid, 64, 84, 118-19

bottle conditioning, 116-17

carbonation and packaging,
115-17

"cask" Kölsch, 117

fermentation, 113-15

filtration, 116

and following recipes, 117-18

homebrew bittering unit
(HBU), 119

hop additions, 118-19

natural carbonation, 98-99,
116-17

pale malted barley, lab
yield, 118

priming sugar, use of, 116-17

racking the beer off, 115

wort as a primer, 116-17

See also Recipes for Kölsch

Hoekkeshouen, Engel, 14

Holy Cross monastery, 11

Homebrew bittering unit
(HBU), 119

Homebrewers, 4-5, 10

Homebrewers (*continued*)
  See also Hobby brewers,
    tips for
Honey, use of, 7, 25
Hop-bitter lager beer, 75
"Hopfenperle," 4
Hoppebier, 4
Hops
  additions of, 118-19
  alpha-acid content, 64, 84,
    118-19
  aroma, 52, 69, 70, 85
  bittering, 51-52, 69, 85
  first use of, 3, 7, 19-20
  German, 46, 63, 68-70, *69,* 85
"Hybrid" style of beer, 60

Indirect heated kiln, 2, 29, 32-33
Industrial Revolution, impact
  of, 29
Isothermally fermented, 55

Jakob. *See* Köbes (waiters)
Jakob Koch, Bier- und
  Malzextrakt-
  Dampfbrauerei, 132-33
Johannis-Bräu, 152
Jungbier (green beer), 31, 96,
  97-98

Kerr Kölsch, 134
Keutebier beers, 3, 19, 20, 25
Kindl, Ernst, 139
Klassic Kölsch, recipe, 121-23
Klatschkies Met Oellich, recipe,
  158-59
Knupp, 31
Köbes (waiter), 105, 107-9, *108*
Koch, Hubert, 132
Kölner Brauhaus
  Vereinsbrauerei, 153
Kölsch beer. *See* Brewing Kölsch;
  Cologne and Kölsch beer;
  Drinking Kölsch; Recipes
  for Kölsch; Sensory profile,
  chemical composition; *spe-
  cific breweries*
Kölsch caviar, 158
Kölsch Konvention
  described, 39-42, *41*
  and drinking beer, 104
  and style parameters, 2-3, 9
Kölsch *wiess,* 32-33, 35, 100
"Kraut" beer, birth of, 6-9
Küppers Brauerei GmbH & Co.
  KG, 143-44
Küppers Kölsch, 143
Kurfürsten-Bräu AG, 144
Kurfürsten-Bräu GmbH, 144-45

Kurfürsten Kölsch, 145
Kurfürsten Maximilian
    Kölsch, 145

Lager beer, 22-23, 26, 35-36,
    125-27
Lag time, 71
Lautering, 77, 78, 83
Lawnmower Kölsch, recipe,
    120-21
Light Kölsch, 49, 148
Liquor to grist ratio, 79

Magnus, Albertus, 18
Malt mill (Malzmühle), 24, 132
Maltose rest, 79-80
Malts
    cooking of, 32
    and grain bill, 63, *64*, 64-
        68, *66*
    production, 24
    speciality, 50
Malzmühle (malt mill), 24, 132
Märzer beers, 31
Mashing
    decoction, 51, 75, 76, 78,
        81-83
    multitemperature infusion
        mash program, 79-80

pH, 71, 72
programs, 77-83
single-infusion, 75, 78, 80-81
step mash program, 76, 77-83
techniques, 75-77
Mead beers, 3, 7
Menu *(foderkaat),* 157
Middle Ages, 16-25
Monastic brewing, 6-7, 10-11, 13
Monheimer Brauerei Peters &
    Bambeck, 145-46
Mt. Hood hops, 70
Multitemperature infusion mash
    program, 79-80
Muuzemandeln, recipe, 162-63

Natural carbonation, 98-99,
    116-17
Nineteenth-Century Hop-Bitter
    Lager Beer, recipe, 125-27
North American pale malts, 68
Northern Brewer hops, 69
"Nosewarmer" (pipe), 30
Nürnberg hop market, *69*

Obergärige Hausbrauerei
    Päffgen, 146-47
Original gravity (OG), 46-48, 49
Oxidation, 77, 78

Index

Packaging
  in bottles, 28, 99, *100,* 101, 102
  in cans, *101,* 101-2
  as draft, 53-54
Päffgen, Hermann, 147
Päffgen Kölsch, 147
Pale beers, 1-2, 25-34
Pentanedione levels, 61
Perle hops, 52, 69, 85
pH/acidity, 52-53
Pilsner beers, 33, 42, 48, 50, 100
Pinten (beer mug), *105,* 105-6
Political issues, 18-19
Porcelain saucers, 110, *111*
Precipitation, 71
Pressure fermentation, 93-94
Priming sugar, use of, 116-17
Primus, Jan (Gambrinus), 16-17, *17*
Privatbrauerei Gaffel Becker & Co., 148-50, *149*
Privat-Brauerei Heinrich Reissdorf GmbH & Co., 150-51, *151*
Privatbrauerei Robert Metzmacher KG, 152-53
Privatbrauerei Sester GmbH & Co. KG, 153-54

Protein rest, 82
Proteins, 65
Publican, 112
Pubs, 30-31, 110, 112. *See also* *specific breweries*
Purity laws, 20-21

Racking the beer off, 115
Rats-Kölsch, 152-53
Recipes for Cologne cuisine. *See* Cologne's classic cuisine
Recipes for Kölsch
  American-Style Kölsch, 123-25
  Bonn-Bonn Kölsch, 127-28
  Klassic Kölsch, 121-23
  Lawnmower Kölsch, 120-21
  Nineteenth-Century Hop-Bitter Lager Beer, 125-27
  See also Brewing Kölsch
Reinheitsgebot, 20, 47
Reissdorf, Carl, 151
Reissdorf, Heinrich, 150
Reissdorf Kölsch, 151
Repitching yeast, 90
Residual alkalinity, water, 70-73
Rheinische Bürger Bräu GmbH & Co. KG, 134, 154-55

Richmodis-Bräu vorm. Brauhaus Friedrich Winter, 155-56
Rievkooche, recipe, 159-60

Saaz hops, 70
Saccharification rest, 80
Saccharomyces cerevisiae (top-fermenting yeast), 60, 73-74
Saccharomyces uvarum (bottom-fermenting yeast), 60
Schankbier, 47, 50
Schlossbrauerei Brühl AG, 142
Schnelle, 106, *106*
Schopen, Peter, 131
Schopen, Wilhelm, 131
Schreckenskammer Kölsch, 143
Sensory profile, chemical composition
   acetaldehyde concentrations, 61
   acetoin, 61
   alcohol content, 48-50, 72
   aroma profile, 59-60
   attenuation, 46, 48-49, 91
   bitter units (BU), 51-52
   of bottled Kölsch, 53
   carbonation, 53-54
   "clean" ale, 60
   color, straw-gold, 45, 50-51

   commonalities among Kölsch, 45-46
   and decoction mashing, 51
   diacetyl, 60-61, 63, 65, 72, 94
   of draft Kölsch, 53-54
   esters, 63, 94
   ethyl-acetate, 59-50
   fermentation by-products, 54-61, 71-72
   filtering, 46, 72, 116
   flavor profile, 59-50
   hops, 46, 51-52
   "hybrid" style, 60
   isothermally fermented, 55
   original gravity (OG), 46-48, 49
   pentanedione levels, 61
   pH/acidity, 52-53
   Saccharomyces cerevisiae (top-fermenting yeast), 60, 73-74
   Saccharomyces uvarum (bottom-fermenting yeast), 60
   top-fermentation, 45, 51
   2-aceto-lactate, 61
   2-phenyl ethanol, 58-59
   yeasts, aroma profile, 59-61
   yeasts, fermentation by-products, 55-57
Sester Kölsch, 154

Sheet filters, for clarification, 99

Siegtal brewery, 139

Silica gels, stabilizing agents, 99

"Simple beer," 4

Single-infusion mashing, 75, 78, 80-81

Sion brewery, 37

Sion Kölsch, 129-30

Soorbrode (sauerbraten), recipe, 160-61

Spalt hops, 69, 85

Sparging, 79, 83

Stabilizing agents, 99-100

Stammtisch, 31

Standard Reference Method (SRM), 51

    See also European Brewery Convention (EBC)

Stange, 103-6, 104

Steckenalt, 31

Steffens Brauerei, 154

Step mash program, 76, 77-83

Stern-Brauerei Carl Funke, 138

"Stood in the chalk," 110

Sünner, Christian, 141

Sweeteners, use of, 66

Tabernash Brewing Company, 73, 74, 76

Tannins, 71

Taxation, 18-21, 23, 36

Temperatures, fermentation, 91-92, 113-14

Tettnang hops, 52, 69, 85

Thousand-bomb attack (Cologne), 37-38

Top-cropping yeast, 74-75, 97

Top-fermentation, 45, 51

Top-fermenting yeast (Saccharomyces cerevisiae), 60, 73-74

2-aceto-lactate, 61

2-phenyl ethanol, 58-59

Unions, 28, 28

Unit conversion chart, 164-65

United Cologne Brewery, 153

Unter Tashenmacher brewery, 37

Vessels for fermentation, 92-93

Vollbier, 47, 50

Waiter (Köbes), 105, 107-9, 108

Water, Kölsch, 63, 70-73

Weihenstephan yeast bank, 74

Wheat, 7, 67-68

Whirlpool rest, 85

Wiess beers, 32-33, 35, 100

Winter, Friedrich, 155-56
Winter Doppel-Märzen, 156
Winter Münchener, 156
Winter Pilsencr, 156
Wood chips, for clarification, 99
World War I and II, impact of,
    34-39
Wort
    boiling and hopping, 83-87,
        84, 86
    as a primer, 116-17
"Written up," 110

Yeasts
    and aroma profile, 59-61
    bottom-fermenting
        (*Saccharomyces uvarum*), 60

bottom harvesting, 74-75, 97
brewing with, 63, 73-75
cropping, 90, 94
and fermentation by-products,
    55-57
nonflocculating, 96, 99
pitching, 89-91
repitching, 90
top-cropping, 74-75, 97
top-fermenting
    (*Saccharomyces cerevisiae*),
    60, 73-74

Zum Kranz, 145
Zum Schiffgen Brewery, 141
Zunft Kölsch, 139
Zur Bretzel, 149-50

About the Author

After completing his Diplom-Braumeister degree from the Technical University of Munich-Weihenstephan in 1990, Eric Warner launched his brewing career when in 1993 he cofounded Tabernash Brewing Company in Denver, Colorado—one of the best and most authentic producers of German-style beers.  In 1997 he moved on to new challenges and accepted the position of vice president of operations at Denver's Broadway Brewing Company.

Warner is author of the Classic Beer Style Series book, *German Wheat Beer,* and has also written numerous articles on brewing and brewery operations. He lives in the Denver area with his wife, Kristin, and their sons, Aidan and Ian. In his spare time, Warner enjoys fly-fishing, hiking, hunting, and skiing. For those of you who read the author biography for *German Wheat Beer,* tennis has been supplanted by the more sedentary country club game of golf; homebrewing has given way to commercial brewing (although it would be great to actually really brew beer again); and yes, the faithful canine companion, Supai, is alive and well at age 12.